From
CHAINS
to
CHANGE

What Grace House Taught Me About Recovery

STEPHEN K. VALLE
with **Marissa J. Elliot**

From Chains to Change
by Stephen K. Valle with Marissa J. Elliott

©2022 Stephen K. Valle
All Rights Reserved
V.2

All rights reserved. No part of this publication may be reproduced, stored in a retrieval system or transmitted in any form, or by any means (electronic, mechanical, photocopying, recording or otherwise) without the prior written permission of the author and the publisher.

This work depicts actual events in the life of the author as truthfully as recollection permits. While all persons within are actual individuals, some names and identifying characteristics have been changed to respect their privacy.

Published by: Nicasio Press,
               Sebastopol, California
               www.nicasiopress.com
Cover design: Steve Kuhn
Author photo: Suzanne Ward-Smith

ISBN: 979-8-9864045-3-0

To my grandchildren, Marissa's children:
Arwen Isabella Elliott and Kaiden Walker Elliott

Table of Contents

Foreword i
Introduction 1
1. "Sir, We Don't Give Up" 11
2. Grace House: My Second Calling 15
3. Breath by Breath 37
4. "Grace Always Bats Last" 43
5. Inside Grace House 71
6. Passing Through the Trap 91
7. Ubuntu: I Am Because We Are 111
8. "I'm Me Again" 123
9. Solstice 133
10. Alex 153
11. Dollar Man 181
12. "Don't Stop Believin'" 199
Acknowledgments 223
Appendix 1. Resources 229
Appendix 2. Accountability 231
About the Author 243
Endnotes 245

Foreword

Offering a foreword to *From Chains to Change: What My Grace House Journey Taught Me About Recovery* is a very welcome task. As someone who spent his career in community corrections in Massachusetts, retiring as acting commissioner in 2013, I developed a visceral understanding of the role addiction plays in tearing apart lives and communities and how difficult it is to find strategies that work. Without effective interventions for probationers with substance use, trauma, and co-occurring mental disorders, all other efforts for changing lives would be unavailing.

It was my good fortune to work with Dr. Steve Valle for years, to learn from him, and to support programming based on his principles. Now the wisdom of a lifetime can be shared through Steve's splendid volume—and not a moment too soon.

Amidst the darkness of the relentless drug crisis, there is some new, hopeful, and critically needed light. Dr. Valle, who has been working at the frontlines of substance misuse intervention for over four decades, has written a career capstone volume offering—if we can only heed it—a clear path forward toward a more humane and effective approach to rescuing people with addictions from their death spiral and helping them to find a new and healthy path forward.

Valle's book is, more than anything else, a captivating and readable story, encapsulating his own personal journey, his experiences with the countless numbers of people with addictions to whom he has dedicated his career, and the model that his experiences and his dialogical approach to treatment led him to develop. In this story—a tale of triumphs and tragedies, personal and professional, that is an up-close and granular look at the world of substance use, trauma, and co-occurring mental disorders—Valle doesn't flinch from the reality of his work, and the reader doesn't have the luxury of looking away. The account here is not presented in the antiseptic language of overly academic treatments but provides a narrative of lives lived and lost, footholds on healthy living achieved amidst setbacks and losses, and enough recovery and redemptions chronicled to give hope for a different future.

What particularly can be learned from this outstanding volume? First and foremost, the troubled men and women struggling with addiction and their family members and friends who desperately want to help can take the stories of Pat, Elvira, Mr. Reliable, and Omar—and Steve—and so many others and understand that they are not alone, left to the mercy of a disease that can be so unforgiving and relentless. They can take heart that, given the desire and the availability of a coherent treatment strategy, health and hope can be restored and lives reclaimed. The stories Valle relates so poignantly tell us of so many apparently intractable cases where, despite the odds, men and women emerge as the living proof that good interventions and treatments can succeed. These stories give hope.

Intervention and treatment providers—dedicated folks who do some of the most difficult work there is—can draw on the experiences catalogued here, especially from

Valle's Accountability Training recovery and change system, a three-pronged approach to intervention and treatment that evolved over decades of frontline experience and that works a fine balance between three key dimensions: accountability, community, and respect. As Valle shares, his change model is not static but dynamic. Thus, the core characteristic of respect, the foundational building block for his model, evolved to include other characteristics of emotional sobriety and spirituality. These dimensions, as Valle reveals to us most poignantly, are delivered by peers helping their peers.

It is the shame of the helping professions and those who do related research and policy development that so little time is spent in dialogue with those who are being treated. It is an oversight born of arrogance and an unspoken disregard for the insights of those who are struggling yet who understand the path to recovery better than the "experts" do. No leading private company would similarly ignore its customers or clients; rather, they would be in constant communication with them, eliciting ideas for product or service improvement and insights as to new directions. So often in the public sector, attending to the voice of the client is overlooked, and with it, opportunities for greater effectiveness are lost.

It could be asked, if those struggling with addiction understand the dynamics involved and see what needs to change, why do they need help? As Valle shows in repeated and striking vignettes, it is because those in the throes of addiction need support and help and, in one of Valle's key insights, a community surrounding them as a reinforcer and a safety net. External accountability—

another building block of Valle's model—is also vital until internal accountability takes hold. And then there is Grace House, his former residence, which Valle created built on hope and a belief in the prospect of recovery. It is a sanctuary for people with addictions, where they can count on each other for understanding and support and can submit willingly to a regimen of mutual accountability and high standards. It is Valle's greatest legacy, a model that drew the attention of White House officials and serves as a beacon for communities nationwide searching for better approaches to the plague of addiction.

Very importantly, in addition to providers and clients, there is one last group for whom this volume can be a transformational learning experience: legislators and key government officials. We are losing ground to the scourge of drug abuse. Despite truly admirable work being done in the trenches by dedicated individuals, existing paradigms for policy and practice need a thorough rethinking. That is why *From Chains to Change* is so timely. Beleaguered communities and disheartened officials—those who control the levers of legislative change and funding decisions—can find here the elements of a path forward. The Accountability Training change model, built from hard-earned experience and informed by those who understand the problem best, and the miracles of Grace House and other peer-driven recovery homes are pillars that can support a new structure for intervention, a light to push back against the current darkness.

Ronald P. Corbett, Jr., EdD
University of Massachusetts Lowell

Introduction

Sailing is one way of illustrating the law of three. A sailboat moves through the water because of the interplay of the wind on its sails (first force) and the resistance of the water against its keel (second force). But to move forward, a third force is required: the destination or heading decided by the helmsperson, who determines the proper set of the sail and the positioning of the keel. The desired goal, moving forward, only occurs if all three forces are engaged.

Solstice is defined as "one of the two times during the year when the sun is farthest north or south of the equator."[1] It is a marker for endings and new beginnings. And it is also the name of the racing sailboat, moored in the classic New England sailing town of Marblehead, Massachusetts, I crewed on during my period of living with, and through, an excruciatingly painful and despair-ridden clinical depression.

This three-to-five-year period of fighting through the trauma-induced turmoil caused by the relentless and baffling pervasiveness of acute and chronic anxiety, loss, and grief fueled the onset of my depression. It was debilitating. The super-confident, high-achieving, leadership-driven self I once knew was slipping away into a shell of my former self. I felt alone even though I was surrounded by solid friends and the support of siblings with whom I felt safe to share my vulnerabilities. Other colleagues and friends provided support, without really knowing what was going on within me; they just knew I wasn't the same Steve they had known. They didn't ask questions or judge. They were just present. Friends do just that: they are present, in person or distantly, when needed most. I knew that, like my crewmates on the *Solstice*—and the life preservers stowed in the cabin, if needed—I could draw on my friends to hold me up and keep me afloat amidst the sea of storms swarming inside of me. I had a community of support to keep me from drowning.

Yet I still felt isolated in a suffocating, emotional quicksand, where every move I tried to make to get myself out of this hole of despair seemed to sink me further into the depths of the darkness. I was stuck in the immobilization of crippling anxiety and the oxygen-sucking energy drain of clinical depression. I was living under one continuous, foreboding shadow. Inwardly, I was beaten down. At times, I was barely able to put one foot in front of the other as I fought to keep up with the demands of being the CEO of a Massachusetts-based behavioral healthcare company for a leading addiction treatment system of care. Somehow, I managed to continue working and being productive, but I was a wounded helper. I felt weak and powerless to do anything but hold onto the shaky cliffs hovering over the pit of despair in which I was immersed. It was my darkest solstice.

Ultimately, I learned the powerful effects that a community of supportive peers can have for healing. I drew on the bonds created among the salty racing crew of the *Solstice*, the teamwork of racing, as well as the unconditional support afforded me by the residents of Grace House. Those residents had the lived experience of battling through the adversity of substance misuse, co-occurring mental health disorders, incarceration, and trauma. Whether our community is large or small, near or far, in person or connected by social media, we all need and thrive in a context where we feel supported and nurtured.

The community of flawed humans at Grace House, most of whom had criminal justice system involvement, became a life preserver in my time of darkness. Like the mooring of the *Solstice*, I was tethered from drifting into the abyss of emotional nothingness by the community of caring and supportive residents at Grace House. I was battered about and worn but still connected. Being connected to a caring community of others who shared excruciating loss and pain was my lifeline, even though much of society preferred to keep these flawed humans out of sight and mind. At Grace House, I saw them in their day-to-day struggles and felt a deep sense of respect and awe for what they had to endure. For them, it took tremendous courage and resilience each day to resist falling back into the web of past criminal behaviors and active addiction. *How did they do this?* I often asked myself. And yet many did. I saw miracle after miracle unfold as they said yes to being respectful of themselves and others. In attaining sobriety once again, their dignity was restored, and their criminal behavior ceased—one day at a time. It was inspirational then, and it is to this day.

Grace House was originally my home in Lynn, Massachusetts, where I lived with my wife and daughter. Since our daughter would be starting kindergarten the next year, we decided it was time to put the house up for sale and move to a less urban community. The neighborhood was challenging, yet the house was grand: a large Victorian with one nine-room owner's apartment and four one- and two-bedroom apartments. It would catch a good price on the emerging real estate market in Lynn, I thought.

I've always felt that my choice, at age twenty-three, to begin my career in the field of alcoholism treatment was a calling, because it was not a career path that young professionals were encouraged to pursue at that time. But I did choose it, and I loved working with people who were seeking recovery from alcoholism and drug addiction. For more than twenty years, I pursued my career with the passion of someone called to their work. Then I had a second calling: to forego the selling of my house and embark on an experiment in resocialization, helping others to help themselves. I had a resource (my house) and an intense desire to make a difference by helping people along their path of recovery and change. I took my house off the market and renamed it Grace House.

I didn't want to run the house myself or take a professional role there. I was okay with coaching and supporting, but I believed that any lasting change for residents would come from them helping and supporting each other. With a few cardinal rules to start—including no use of alcohol or drugs or any act of violence toward others while a resident—I began teaching the residents the principles of my Accountability Training change model. Grace House had no staff present to keep order, provide structure, or be called upon for help in problem-solving around the issues of early recovery from addiction and mental health disorders. They had to be their own staff. I remained in the background and kept a distant eye on how things were going, but it was their job to operate a safe housing environment for themselves, using the tools I taught them.

Most of the residents in early recovery were also under probation or parole supervision or recently released from jail or prison. Some came from other treatment programs, hospitals, or social service programs and had been able to avoid being arrested or caught up in criminal behavior. Though they came from all walks of life and backgrounds, they had the commonality of struggling with addiction, co-occurring mental health disorders, and/or trauma and yearned to be freed from the bondage and pain of these disorders.

From my background in designing and operating professional substance use disorder and addiction programs for similar populations around the country, I realized that professional intervention and treatment programs have their flaws. As good as many programs are, they still miss something essential. There is a gap in the connectedness between professional program staff and participants. This gap, or boundary, is an essential component of professional programs and exists for a variety of valid reasons. It is a necessary limitation.

However, I've always felt this gap needs a bridge. Grace House became that bridge. Like the galvanized steel cables of a suspension bridge, the peer group was what it took to keep the bridge intact.

Grace House was entirely peer run. It was supported by the residents paying their own rent; keeping order among the divergent, unpredictable, and sometimes volatile mix of personalities and backgrounds; and being responsible for the upkeep and maintenance of the house. There were no government grants or contracts or professional staff to rely on for assistance or to monitor the residents' behavior. I challenged this community of splintered lives to be their own clinical staff, their own probation and parole officer, and accountable to their own peer community of residents in the shared living environment. This they did for more than two decades, with me providing guidance and support, as needed. I was the "rational authority" to whom they could turn, but it was the peers who ran the house. Ultimately, it was I who needed them.

Through the process of living among this community of peers as part of my own recovery process, I became connected to the residents at Grace House in a different manner. Though they insisted on calling me "the Doc," I was now their peer, living through similar emotional pain. They saw me as vulnerable and hurting, yet they made no judgments. With the caring and support of these wounded healers, I emerged out of the darkness and into a new solstice arising. The life lessons I learned from initially mentoring these residents—first as an outside professional who was there to offer support and encouragement, and then as a peer during my own period of emotional pain—are the driving forces behind this book.

This community of former inmates and court-involved people seeking refuge at Grace House, flawed and wounded as they were, became my life preserver and my purveyors of healing. In becoming unglued and humbled by the failures in my personal life, and then being blindsided by the resulting emotional downspin of depression, I experienced firsthand the transformational power of peers helping peers. My four decades of living and working among people afflicted with and affected by drugs, alcohol, trauma, and co-occurring mental health disorders helped me formulate my Accountability Training peer-to-peer behavior change model.

At Grace House, I embarked on a journey of creating hope for those deemed hopeless by others. It was an experiment in resocialization, relying on the power of peer *accountability* and the connectedness provided by one's *community of peers*. As I observed over time, when that community is characterized by *respect* for oneself and others, transformational change happens.

The law of three was articulated most prominently in the early twentieth century work of G. I. Gurdjieff, a "one-of-a-kind spiritual genius." The Armenian-born spiritual teacher founded a new stream of contemporary esotericism known as the "Gurdjieff work."[2] The law of three, a fundamental cosmic law, states that every whole phenomenon is composed of three separate sources or forces. This law of three applies to everything in the universe and humanity, including structures and processes.

Gurdjieff taught his students to think of law of three forces as essential to transforming the energy of the human being. This process of transformation requires the three forces of affirming (active), denying (passive), and reconciling (neutral).[3] A core tenet of the law of three is that the interweaving of these three forces creates a fourth new dimension: a new arising. "Whenever there is an authentic new arising, the Law of Three is somehow involved."[4]

The Accountability Training change model I created is based on a new law of three that, rather than positive/negative/neutral forces, describes three forces key for recovery from addiction, co-occurring mental health disorders, and trauma. This model evolved from my interactions with offenders in our treatment programs in jails, prisons, and court-based initiatives and through the interactions and relationships I formed when I went through my own recovery process at Grace House. According to this new law of three, transformational change, sustained over time, is attainable when the three interdependent forces of *accountability, community*, and *respect* are all at play. When these three forces are interwoven into one's lifestyle and important relationships, a new arising occurs that fuels the transformational change process. This book is about those who influenced me and who put into practice (often even without knowing it) this new law of three, which propelled us—and countless others who participated in programs I operated in various jails, prisons, and community corrections settings—into a life of meaningful change.

The United States is the world leader of opioid prescribing, opioid addiction, and opioid overdose deaths. The drug overdose public health and public safety epidemic in this country is claiming 185 lives a day and costs over $1 trillion annually.[5] Drug-overdose deaths reached record numbers during the COVID-19 pandemic, eclipsing a hundred thousand annually for the first time in American history.[6]

The threat of illicit drugs to our American way of life and sense of security has risen to the level where it has been declared a national emergency.[7] At the same time, a report issued by the surgeon general found that rates of depression, anxiety, impulse behavior, and attempted suicide have all risen among children and adolescents.[8] It is impossible to grasp the enormity of this reality…until it becomes your reality as a loved one or as a victim.

And yet, as I learned from the residents at Grace House during my own recovery process, and from graduates of programs where the Accountability Training model was used, the statistics don't define us. We have every reason to hope. Hope is the most compelling reason of all to share these stories with you. Recovery and transformational change can and do occur. My goal in writing this memoir is for all of us, individually and collectively, to discover untold new arisings as we integrate the forces of accountability, community, and respect of self and others into our personal lives, our relationships, and society. It is time to reset the conversation.

From Chains to Change

1

"Sir, We Don't Give Up"

"I've never seen it like this! In all my years on the street, it's never been so bad. It's crazy. Kids, adults, doesn't matter—they're all dropping like flies. It's never been like this, Doc. I don't know if I can take it. It's really killing me. On our own doorstep, Doc! No warning. Nothing. And the kid is down!"

Pat was calling me as I was going through the Ted Williams Tunnel in Boston. He had lived at Grace House for more than ten years and had grown into a peer mentor and house president. Our mobile phone connection wasn't great. "Hang on, buddy. I might lose you," I said.

Ironic, I thought to myself. When it's a matter of survival, the life of a Grace House guy is all about connection—literally as well as figuratively.

The human bond among those who have survived the trauma of incarceration and the crazy maze of our criminal justice system, along with the bondage of drug addiction and co-occurring mental health disorders and trauma, is like no other. It's stronger than the cement walls and barbed wire fencing encircling the perimeter of our more than six thousand prisons and jails. By contrast, there are only about four thousand colleges and universities in the United States. Think about that. We have more prisons and jails than we have colleges and universities of higher education. Ouch.

"I'm out of the tunnel, Pat. What's going on?" I pulled over so I could take notes while I listened to Pat recount his version of what just went down at Grace House.

It went something like this: "So, Doc, this kid shows up on the front doorstep. I don't know him or nothing. But I hear banging, so I run to see what's going on. You never know what's going down, living on the Lynn Commons, right? I open the door, and bam! The kid goes down. He collapses. He's out. I see the look, and I know."

Pat explained that some guys were standing nearby on the steps of Grace House. They'd heard the commotion this kid made, so he yelled at them to get the Narcan, quick. "But they just freeze, Doc," he continued. "So I run and get the Narcan. I administer it, and the kid's back. He gathers himself, and then he takes off. No 'thank you' from him. He looks at me and nods, but he just takes off."

I stopped taking notes for a minute so I could let Pat know I was hearing him. I asked if that was the last time he saw the kid.

"Yeah," he said. "He probably knew the cops would get there soon. And he was right. A squad car from the Commons pulled up. 'We saw what went down,' the officers said. 'You just saved that kid's life, you know.'"

I confirmed that's exactly what Pat did. And I asked if he knew the kid.

"No. None of us knew this kid. But we've lost a lot in the last few years we did know. I mean, thank God, not in the house. But after they left. They make it for a while, and then we have another funeral to go to. Things have changed, Doc. It's bad out there. They say, 'Relapse is part of the disease.' But these days, you relapse. And you die. How many do we have to bury, Doc?"

This hit me in the gut. *He's so right*, I thought.

The opioid drug overdose epidemic is changing the public safety and public health landscape—and that of individual families who have a loved one with an untreated addiction and resulting brain impairment—more quickly than I've witnessed over the entire course of my forty-year career in the alcohol and drug treatment field. It is very different today than it was when I began my career. But the most dramatic changes have occurred in the past twenty years, since the turn of the century.

For many, addiction is a relapsing disease, for sure. But unlike in previous eras, relapse in these times, when drugs on the streets are laced with fentanyl or other synthetic opioids, often results in death. Opioids account for three-quarters of all drug overdose deaths.[9] The statistics are painful and paralyzing. But then there are those connections, those reasons to fight back and change the newspaper headlines.

Two days after he saved a child's life—because that is what he did: he saved a child from a fiendish drug—Pat went to get an Italian sub after work. While he was waiting for his order at a sub shop not far from Grace House, he was approached by a police officer.

The cop said, "We heard what you did the other day. That was good stuff. We've been talking a lot about it at the station. We have a recovery coach working out of the Lynn Police Department now. Can I give him your name and number so you guys can connect? We need a lot of foot soldiers in this battle. We're glad you're part of the team."

Pat was fully on board with this. "We'll help anyone, sir," he said. "Many may not be ready for help, like that kid the other day. But we don't give up. Tell your recovery coach to stop by any time."

After he'd paid for his sub, Pat told the officer, "We used to run from you guys. Now we're running with you. We're no longer out to hurt others. We're here to help those folks who are still where we once were." He smiled as he picked up his sub from the counter, and added, "That's what we do at Grace House. Have a good day, sir."

2

GRACE HOUSE: MY SECOND CALLING

It was an early Sunday morning, before the neighborhood had awoken from its usual Lynn Commons Saturday night hangover, when I noticed two people standing in front of my house. They were looking down at the sidewalk on the corner of Mall Street and North Common Street. My daughter, who was four years old, was playing inside and getting ready to go to church in Marblehead. I went over to say good morning to the two people, and as I did, they looked at me and shook their heads. A caulk outline of a dead body branded the sidewalk right in front of my house.

"This neighborhood is getting bad. It's not safe anymore, especially for kids," they said, and they were right.

When I saw the outline, I shuddered. And I knew instantly I had to move my family out of the neighborhood. Months before, I had pulled a gun from out of the front hedge. The year before that, we'd had a break-in and robbery. I wasn't sure what I should do with the house. At that point, one of my options was to operate it as a rental property, as we had four units with tenants in them as well as my office space. Or I could sell the property completely and move on.

I talked to a broker and let her know we'd be putting the house on the market soon. We wanted to move in time for my daughter to start kindergarten in the Marblehead school system, where we were hoping to find our new home. Of course, I would miss our current house. It was a grand turn-of-the-century structure that was once home to one of Lynn's shoe industry magnates. Lynn Commons, with its trees, walking paths, gazebo, and grass fields, was vibrant and full of culturally diverse activity. It was a friendly and stimulating place. I loved taking walks, carrying my daughter on my shoulder and singing to her, as friendly neighbors from all ethnic backgrounds greeted us with warm smiles and congratulatory nods. Though many did not speak English, the joy of a dad carrying his child is something people with all cultures, ethnicities, and languages can celebrate. Living in Lynn was very much like my Yonkers upbringing in that regard. Indiscriminate threats of violence were not acceptable, and I knew that as much as I might value the environment, safety had to be our first priority.

I had been on the advisory board of the Salvation Army Rehabilitation Program (Sally's) for several years, along with other members of the Lynn area business community, including the president of a local bank. One of the owners of the hospital where I was chief of psychology—my first appointment after receiving my doctorate from Boston University—had opened the door for me to meet Larry King (not the Larry King of CNN fame), the president of the Saugus Bank and Trust (now

Eastern Bank). The opportunity to serve together on the Sally's advisory board furthered a developing relationship of respect and trust and illustrated one of the principles that would shape my work and my approach with people in various stages of change. Connectedness and support from others are needed in all stages of life. Mentors, coaches, teachers, colleagues, friends, and community all help us be connected in a way that creates belonging. We need each other. No one was meant to go it alone. Individuals with addiction and co-occurring mental health disorders, criminal offenders, those still incarcerated or under court supervision, and those released from prison or jail need what all of us need: connection with others who can have a positive influence in our lives.

I had professional standing with my doctoral credentials and job as chief of psychology, so on the outside, I portrayed an air of confidence and strength. On the inside, I was full of anxiety, doubt, and insecurity. I was unprepared for the business world I found myself in. My dad often said he couldn't advise me, but he always led me back to the Bible to search for the direction he felt inadequate to give. The Bible and *Pilgrim's Progress* were the only books I recall seeing him read. He spoke three languages and could read four, but he only had five years of formal schooling, so he would express his inadequacy at being able to provide guidance for me. He encouraged me to study the scriptures and to seek advice from others about how to traverse the business world he had never been exposed to. His inability to help me left me drifting. Yet, over time, I came to appreciate his willingness to be open about his vulnerability and limitations. He displayed the wisdom of knowing, by not knowing.

Mr. King liked my entrepreneurial drive and work ethic, though I had no asset base other than my potential. He granted my first loan to launch my consulting business and private clinical practice out of my home on North Common Street. I also obtained the mortgage to finance my home from this bank. A few years later, when I changed its purpose from being my personal residence to being a residence for ex-cons and others in recovery, that understandably raised some eyebrows in the mortgage department. With the support of the bank president and my personal guarantees to secure the loan (I had no idea what that meant at the time, though I was learning to put trust and faith into action), the tentative vision I had of the house being converted began to take shape in my mind. I knew I didn't want to develop another treatment program, even though there was a great need for more such programs, both in justice settings and in healthcare. This remains true today, with the opioid overdose crisis across America. Developing and implementing programs was what I did for a living. Even though owning a private treatment program could be lucrative, I had a sense this wasn't the answer. Rather, I was interested in an alternative that bridged the gap between incarceration, a court program, residential treatment in a hospital or rehabilitation center, and independent living. It needed to be something outside the norm of traditional provider-driven options, but what was the "it"?

That "it," I learned later, was Grace House. Like the sense of calling I'd had when I took my first executive position in the alcoholism and drug treatment field decades earlier, this was my second calling.

I put the brakes on selling my home, sensing something more meaningful than a real estate capital gain was possible. I decided to secure a mortgage for my new home in Marblehead before selling the North Common Street property. This gave me the option and the time to keep the vision that was percolating in my mind conceptually alive.

Or so I thought.

Though not my preference, I bought more time by pursuing the conventional route of getting approval from the Department of Public Health Bureau of Substance Abuse Services to create a transitional living facility. I thought starting there would generate the least resistance from the NIMBY ("not in my backyard") folks. I researched the various options for licensing approval and consulted with the Massachusetts Bureau of Substance Abuse Services. The state authorities advised me that the physical plant most likely fit the category of a licensed halfway house. I was informed that my first step was to get approval from the local zoning authority. Several residents in early recovery were already living there, so I was in compliance with the zoning regulations for an apartment-house dwelling.

However, it was clear to me that the residents, who were recently discharged from a treatment program or from jail, were not ready for the freedom afforded by the layout of the five-unit building. Without supervision and no one to hold them accountable, I feared it wouldn't be long before one or more of the tenants ended up using alcohol and drugs again. My fears were not unfounded. Renting to individuals in early recovery without any accountability was not working well. In fact, it was a nightmare. I had been stiffed on the rent more than a few times. One tenant even pried off the turn-of-the century marble fireplace mantle and façade and sold it for drugs. That same tenant sued me for discriminating against him when I wouldn't let him return to the apartment. I was amazed that a lawyer would even take the case. Nothing came of the lawsuit, as you would expect, because it was a ploy to squeeze money from me by getting me to agree to a potential settlement.

Going Toe-to-Toe With the Lynn City Council

Given my failed attempts at renting to individuals trying to stay sober on their own, it made sense to obtain a license for a halfway house program. This would offer the residents the staff support they needed to sustain their early recovery goals. It wasn't what I ultimately wanted to do—which was to begin a new type of program—but it was a first step. I proposed to the Lynn City Council that they approve my application to the Bureau of Substance Abuse for a licensed halfway house. I would convert three of the apartments into one congregate housing unit that could accommodate about twelve residents. The other two apartments could be used as independent graduate apartments. I argued that, as a licensed facility, it would be staffed by professionals and have twenty-four-hour supervision by paid staff. The neighbors would be assured that a professional staff member would be present to handle any active drug use or other problems that might arise. In a neighborhood that was known for drug dealing and violence, I thought a program with professional staff providing on-site supervision would be greeted with open arms as a means to stabilize the neighborhood.

I was dead wrong.

Except for two councilors on the Lynn City Council, my pleas fell on deaf ears. Most of the council members held fast to the zoning restrictions that stated no more than three unrelated people could live together without a zoning variance. I argued that a halfway house with supervision would help to stabilize the neighborhood and offer hope to those who wanted to stop drinking and using drugs. One of my neighbors, who was a well-known physician, opposed the project, which was surprising and disappointing to me. Ironically, this same neighbor was busted years later for writing illegal drug prescriptions. In the end, the council voted to deny my application for a zoning variance.

However, that was only round one in my fight. I continued to believe in the transformational power of recovery and change, regardless of one's past mistakes. So I filed an appeal asking the court to issue a summary judgment to overturn the actions of the city council. I was denied again. It was becoming a costly process and beyond my means to fund. Our household income was adequate for a family with one child, but we had little room for expenses beyond our daily living costs. Teachers, like my wife, were underpaid in the mid-1980s, and I was just starting my career as a psychologist. It seemed my only option was to walk away and accept defeat. That didn't seem right. The admonition of my dad to follow Micah 6:8 on whatever path I chose in life rang often in my ears: "What doth the Lord require of thee, but to do justly, and to show mercy, and to walk humbly?"[10]

Though the thought of surrendering to an obvious injustice was anathema to me, I could not ignore the economic and political power of the opposition. The most logical option was to sell my house and use the proceeds to move my family to the safer, upscale Marblehead area (where our broker had found a suitable and affordable home close to the schools) and find other ways to be of service there. *What else could I do?* I wondered.

I was in a state of great internal conflict because the principles of fairness, justice, and compassion for others in need, rooted in my Christian upbringing, were important to me. I couldn't just abandon this calling, which was so much a part of who I am. Yet even within my faith, I found conflict. Service to others was a principle nurtured by my experience in a church youth group helping the homeless alcoholic population in New York City. Yet this clashed with the biblical admonition to obey the rules of those in authority. "Render unto Caesar what is Caesar's, and unto God what is God's," Jesus taught his followers. *What was I to do?* Listen to the authorities who told me I could not move forward due to zoning regulations or pursue my calling to "do justice, love mercy, and walk humbly" by creating a house that would help those in need?

I did not have clarity. As a competitor, I didn't like losing, especially when the rules were stacked unequally against the downtrodden. The injustice angered me. Nor was I one to give up, at least not without a fight. I had learned on the streets of Yonkers that the only way to deal with bullying behavior (and I did think the people I was fighting for were being bullied) is to stand up to it. Those experiencing homelessness had no home and thus no voice; I was their only voice, it seemed. I didn't have the money to fight a long court battle—which is what my lawyer advised me it would likely take—to overturn the city council's decision. *I did what I could do*, I told myself. The mental shadowboxing that was tormenting me was fatiguing. My logical mind chirped at me, "It's time to fold."

My heart differed.

What would Jack Sidebotham, my father figure during my teenage years, do? What would Manny Lopes, my first supervisor and longtime mentor, do? What would Harold Hughes, the former governor, senator, and presidential candidate with whom I had become a close confident, do? What would Charlie Powell, the successful entrepreneur who later became my business partner and dearest friend and spiritual mentor, do? These influencers on my life had similar values. They were not bashful about taking on the establishment. They did what they could at the time they were called to do it. They listened to their inner voice, the calling within to defend and to fight for the dignity and respect of others. They listened to their spirituality. They followed their heart.

I chose to do the same. I took the City of Lynn to court.

With the decision to continue to fight, and the long and costly court battle looming, I faced an even more challenging decision: How could I keep alive the housing alternative my home had become for people in early recovery, while waiting for a hearing date from the Massachusetts Superior Court?

On Retreat on the Eastern Shore of Maryland

I was in a no-man's-land waiting for the Superior Court hearing date. Then I traveled to Maryland's Eastern Shore to attend the Big Book/Good Book 12-Step Retreat run by former governor and senator from Iowa Harold Hughes and his friend Charlie Powell, both of whom were in long-term recovery. These two were pivotal figures in furthering my calling to serve, as they had done themselves, those afflicted and affected with alcoholism and drug addiction. Their Eastern Shore retreats were epic in the spiritual development of scores of others from all walks of life and status.

Harold was the type of born-again Christian I could identify with and look up to. He advocated for the rights of Native Americans, alcoholics, drug-addicted persons, and the mentally ill to be treated with respect and to be afforded dignity. He fought against the judgmental and self-righteous attitudes of his evangelical brethren and challenged them not to judge, to be kindhearted and loving, and to serve those less fortunate than themselves. He spoke against Christians who put their religion ahead of the gospel message Jesus had taught and lived. People in places of power in politics and those in positions of influence in business respected Harold, as did those with little or no power. His charismatic personality and compassionate spirit attracted people from all walks of life. As a senator, he sponsored the Comprehensive Alcohol Abuse and Alcoholism Prevention, Treatment, and Rehabilitation Act of 1970. It became known as the Hughes Act. This legislation launched the National Institute on Alcohol Abuse and Alcoholism (NIAAA), which was charged with developing and conducting comprehensive health, education, training, research, and planning programs for the prevention and treatment of alcohol-related problems.

In 1978, Harold was featured in *Born Again*, along with President Nixon's special counsel and hatchet man Chuck Colson. Chuck was named as one of the Watergate Seven and served prison time for his role in the Watergate scandal. He went from the power and prestige of the White House to humiliation of imprisonment in the "Big House." As part of his journey, however, Chuck had a born-again experience, a spiritual awakening, as they call it in AA. Because of this transformative change, he zealously devoted the rest of his life to those in prison, their children, and their families. He founded Prison Fellowship International, which Harold was instrumental in bringing to prominence. I met Chuck at one of Harold's retreats, and his powerful example of what a former presidential advisor and released prisoner could do to help others made a powerful impact on me. He showed great interest in my hopes and dreams for Grace House.

My relationship with Harold evolved into one of mutual trust and collaboration as we joined forces on many governmental projects he sponsored as well as personal interventions he was involved in. When people in high positions in the government and business knew someone they cared for was struggling with an alcohol problem, they called Harold for confidential advice and consultation. He often called me to assist with these high-profile people, who included elected officials, prominent business executives, and their respective family members. Strict confidentiality was critical.

In 1993, Harold nominated me to serve as director of the Federal Substance Abuse and Mental Health Services Administration (SAMHSA) in the Clinton administration. Though I had received a phone call from a White House staff member informing me about my nomination, the next morning, I awoke to news on *Good Morning America* that President Clinton had nominated another candidate. Within the hour, Harold called to say, "Well, Steve, we harnessed a lot of congressional support for you, we won the fight, and you were the nominee. I'm not sure what happened, but it changed overnight. That's politics in Washington. However, the deputy director position is yours if you want it."

I asked if I could think about it for a bit.

He told me to call him back by noon.

It didn't take me long to call him back. "Thanks," I said, "for all you've done for me and the alcoholism field. I'm so humbled and honored to have been your candidate and I appreciate all the support for my candidacy. However, if I'd become the director of SAMHSA, I'd have wanted to choose my own deputy. I think the nominee should have that choice. If she chooses me, I'll be honored to serve."

Harold called me the next day to say the new director had someone else in mind. "Steve," he said, "in the long run, coming in second may be best thing that happened for your career."

He was right. If I had gone to Washington and headed the major federal agency of SAMSHA, I would have had no time or energy to devote to Grace House. I would have moved my family to the DC area and probably would have had to sell Grace House in order to live there. I would have missed out on the relationships that became such a central part of who I am. Though disappointed, I was at peace. I was able to focus on my calling.

At the retreat I attended while waiting for the Massachusetts Superior Court hearing, Harold mentioned to me the work of Paul Molloy, a good friend he had met while serving as senator from Iowa. He shared his thoughts about the Oxford House movement Paul started and how it was gaining momentum across the country. "It may be a way out of your dilemma of waiting for a Superior Court decision," Harold suggested.

Charlie Powell, who was part of this conversation, agreed and encouraged me to pursue Harold's idea. Charlie was never bashful about taking on the bureaucracy, especially when it got in the way of helping people with alcoholism. "Us drunks need you educated types to fight with us too," he said.

"Us drunks" was the term Charlie frequently called himself and others with alcoholism.

"Look into it, Steve," Harold said with his deep and captivating voice, his piercing eyes looking straight at me.

As I drove home from the Eastern Shore over the Chesapeake Bay Bridge, which spans the Chesapeake Bay and connects the state's rural Eastern Shore region with the urban Western Shore, I was in deep contemplation. My heart was beating at a faster clip than normal. I could not erase from my mind Harold's and Charlie's words and their pleading looks. I sensed an unspoken passing of the baton from "two hardcore old drunks" to me as a younger professional. They wanted me to join them in the advocacy movement that was emerging around the country, resulting from Harold's courageous leadership in Congress. They wanted me to be part of the marathon of social justice reforms that would be needed to create better access to healthcare for those with alcohol and drug problems. They needed me to unite with them as a voice from the professional community to advocate for those whose voices were silenced by the shame and pain of their addiction journey. As I approached the Baltimore/Washington International Thurgood Marshall Airport to catch my flight back to Boston, I continued to ponder the exhortation Harold and Charlie had imprinted on my psyche. I sensed the Eastern Shore retreat was unfolding into a mission I was called to carry out in some form, yet to be determined.

The conversations from that retreat and the follow-up actions I took led me to a new strategy. The vague calling I felt about using the Lynn house as a ministry to those in need began to take on form and substance. Could I use my home to establish a self-governing, peer-run sober house that was also sanctioned by federal legislation? If so, this would overrule the local zoning restrictions on more than three unrelated people living together. Wow! Suddenly I had a tool to use in my court battle with the city of Lynn that would strengthen my position of respecting the rights of others in recovery to live together as a family unit, regardless of their past addictions and criminal record.

During this time, Charlie Powell was a constant source of guidance and encouragement, helping me move forward in my calling, even though what I was doing went against the grain of local politics and bureaucracy. "Just do the next right thing, buddy," he told me. "Leave the rest up to the Man upstairs. When you're piloting in the clouds, you've got to trust the instruments. Right? You're in the storm clouds of local politics, and the Good Lord ain't going to let you go off course, not too far anyway. And if you find you're a bit off, and you've done the best you could, He'll provide you with a parachute."

Charlie was an excellent pilot. I often sat in the co-pilot seat of his single-engine turbo-charged jet, so he knew that the piloting metaphor would ring true for me. I had my visual flight reference pilot's license, and I was working on obtaining my instrument rating. I had flown through many clouds, sometimes in but mostly around thunderstorms, with Charlie piloting his plane. He was one cool pilot, especially in the storm clouds. I learned a great deal observing how he trusted his instruments and the controller's instructions, while simultaneously getting tossed around in the turbulence. So his advice to keep on course and trust the instruments of my heart and my faith had meaning.

My lawyer advised me to pursue my vision but to keep a low profile. He said the federal law was clearly on my side, but that didn't mean I wouldn't face a lot of resistance locally if someone wanted to create a problem. He explained that his read of the political tea leaves was that the city solicitor, with the knowledge of the Oxford House legislation (i.e., requiring all states to provide start-up funds for groups to open sober living arrangements based on the Oxford House model) delivered to him by my attorney, was content to let sleeping dogs lie.

"John," I said to my attorney, "that sounds okay, but can I have something in writing from the city solicitor?"

John knew all the city counselors and the local politics; he was a partner in the same law firm as the current mayor. This was the major reason I had selected him as my attorney.

"I don't want to push it, Steve. It's better not to draw attention and have it inevitably tied up in court. You would ultimately win, but it would cost a lot of time—likely years—and significant money. People need the help now, right? I can't advise you on what to do, but legally the ball is in the city's court. My read of the climate is that unless there is a lot of pressure, they are likely to leave it alone for now. If they don't, then we'll fight it, ultimately at the Massachusetts Supreme Court."

So I pressed on, regardless of the impending lawsuit, and opened the doors to Grace House.

Harold Hughes died in 1996, the year I officially opened the doors of Grace House.

A couple of weeks before he passed, we had an inspiring and moving phone conversation. He was quite ill. "Steve, I'm not going to be here that much longer," he said slowly and deliberately. "You have a passion for us drunks that is rare in professionals I've been around. We need young professionals like yourself—people with credentials and a heart—to carry the message of recovery and offer hope to those trapped in the despair and hopelessness of addiction. When I'm not here any longer to fight for folks like us, I know you will. And that gives me great peace." He encouraged me to continue my fight for the rights of people with the disease of addiction and to pursue my vision for Grace House, no matter what resistance I faced.

I vowed to do just that.

Breakthrough: The Oxford House Experiment

As I researched this movement in the early 1990s, I could not find an Oxford House model for released male and female offenders from jail or prison who were living as one family. I felt an adaption of the Oxford House model that also drew on the rules and the tools of the therapeutic community treatment approach I was using in my jail- and prison-based programs would be an ideal match for the released inmates, probationers, and drug-court participants who would find their way to the doorstep of Grace House. Though the male and female residences were separate, I felt residents could function as one self-governing community if they were taught the skills to do so. And they in turn could teach new family members how to live in a community with others, be accountable, and be of service. "Right living, right now" is a well-known mantra stated in staff-run therapeutic community programs in jails and prisons. If it worked in settings with staff supervision, could it not work in a community without staff present?

In 1989, the *Washington Post* published a story on the history of the Oxford House movement, which was growing slowly but steadily around the country.[11] The web page of the Oxford House organization summarizes the history and early growth of Oxford House:

> The first Oxford House was established in 1975 in Silver Spring, Maryland. From the beginning, the group rejected ownership of any property and continues to rent—not purchase—single-family houses in good neighborhoods to establish new Oxford Houses. In the years between 1975 and 1988, eighteen Houses were established by and for recovering individuals. The principles of replication and guidelines for running a group home for recovering alcoholics and substance abusers embodied in the Oxford House Manual had become institutionalized in the Washington, D.C. Metropolitan area, and in 1987, a house for ten men was rented in Bethlehem, PA....
>
> In 1988, Congress enacted P.L. 100-690, the Anti-Drug Abuse Act. This Act included a provision that required all states to establish a revolving loan fund to provide start-up funds for groups wishing to open sober living environments based on the Oxford House model. The mandate was changed to a permissive provision in 1990 and is now codified as 42 USC 300x-25....

By 1991, when the CBS program *60 Minutes* did a favorable ten-minute segment about Oxford House, there were 256 Oxford Houses throughout the country....

Moreover, Oxford House World Services supervised legal actions throughout the country to resolve civil rights with respect to zoning restrictions and the NIMBY problem. In 1995, the United States Supreme Court considered the rights of recovering individuals to rent houses in areas zoned for single-family residence. In its decision in City of Edmonds, WA v. Oxford House, Inc. 514 US 725 (May 15, 1995), the U.S. Supreme Court found that recovering alcoholics and drug addicted persons are protected under the Federal Fair Housing Act as handicapped individuals and local governments must make reasonable accommodations in their local zoning law restrictions. This case laid the foundation for several other cases where courts have prohibited discrimination against recovering individuals living together for the purpose of becoming comfortable enough in sobriety to avoid relapse.[12]

Having heard nothing about my court hearing date and bolstered by the Supreme Court decision in City of Edmonds, WA v. Oxford House, Inc. (May 15, 1995), I broke down the walls that divided the apartments. I created two large residences—one for men and one for women. They would be run following the federally sanctioned guidelines of Oxford House, with an added twist: I would create a therapeutic community model without staff to guide the community; instead, I would teach the residences how to govern themselves.

Essentially, I integrated what I was doing professionally for prison and jail programs throughout the country with the peer-run, self-governing philosophy of Oxford House. I called this experiment in resocialization an Oxford House Plus model. Six hundred Oxford Houses were spread throughout the country, but to my knowledge, none was like the Oxford House Plus model operating at Grace House for primarily male and female released prisoners and the court referred offender population. We received a charter from the Oxford House organization, and Grace House was launched.

Coming up with a name for the house was easy for me. I grew up experiencing "for by grace are you saved through faith, it is the gift of God." Also, at AA meetings in my early career days, one of the banners on the wall that grabbed my attention had the slogan "But for the Grace of God." One of my favorite country hymns sung by Elvis Presley was "Amazing Grace." So it was a natural for me to name the house Grace House, and to have as its logo be "Grace House…It's Amazing."

Unique in Massachusetts, and perhaps in the country at the time, Grace House would focus upon those with criminal justice involvement and be a coed community with separate living residences for men and women. Those early years of the Grace House experiment were energizing and challenging. We established some basic guidelines for the residents. The community members felt that a person needed to have completed a treatment program, preferably one of at least six months in duration, as a prerequisite. I found it interesting that this requirement came from the community itself and was not one of my stipulations. It was a big endeavor with a lot of risk, but we had done what had appeared impossible. We had gotten it started! Now we had to make it work.

From Chains to Change

3

BREATH BY BREATH

"Dr. Valle?"

"Susan, what's wrong?"

"Please come. He's in a rage. Pacing. Yelling. Banging on the bedroom door. I'm scared. I called the police They're on their way."

"Okay, good! Are you okay, Susan? Have you been hurt in any way?"

"No, but I'm terrified he'll lose control. Please, Dr. V, he won't talk to anyone but you."

"Okay, Susan. I'm on my way. I'm getting in my car right now. Are you in a safe place? Where is Omar?"

"He's in the other room. Like I said, pacing, seething, yelling nonsense, slamming cupboards, hitting walls. I can't talk any sense to him."

"Can you give him the phone?"

"I don't know. I'm afraid. I'm in the bedroom, and I told him to stay away."

"Can you slide the phone to him under the door and tell him it's me on the line? Okay? Just stay where you are."

"Yes, I think I can do that…Oh, the police are almost here. The sirens are coming down the street.…"

"Please slide him the phone and tell him it's me."

I waited as muffled sounds suggested the phone was being passed along. "Omar? Can you hear me?"

"Yeah, but they're here, Doc. Four or five squad cars. A bunch of guys with guns. I'm going to go out and tell them to leave us alone. I ain't done nothing wrong, Doc. We can handle our own problems."

"No, Omar, no. Listen to me. Don't go outside. Stay exactly where you are. I'm on my way. I want you to take deep breaths. I'm in the car now. Breathe, Omar. Breathe. And talk to me...*Stay on the phone, Omar! Stay with me!*"

But I couldn't keep him there. You can never force anyone. It is always their choice to make—no matter how much you want to hold them and protect them, like you would your own child.

As I approached the bottom of Adams Street, I could see the reflection of multiple police lights swirling color into the black night. I sped toward the flashing reds and blues and the fear I knew Omar was living.

I pulled over quickly, jerked the vehicle into park, and surveyed the scene. I felt a stinging, sinking feeling in my stomach. I wanted to throw up on the spot. In my mind, it was clear the cops were going to fire at what they saw emerging from the house: a huge Black man, full of rage, waving his arms and about to charge them. Omar was six foot, four inches, and weighed over 275 pounds.

I knew Omar well enough to know he was not armed and was not violent by nature, but the cops had no knowledge of him as a person. They only saw a potentially huge threat approaching them. In a way, it was a perfect, albeit troubling, example of the line we walk every day in corrections and offender treatment programs. On the one hand, officers are trained to react to threats and keep visitors and staff safe. Inmates, on the other hand, are conditioned to survive and to distrust authority. Both stances have validity, and we are always trying to bridge the gap between them.

Bridge that gap. But how do you bridge it in moments of life and death? There is no time for the cross-training of correctional and clinical staff that would allow them to determine the best practices to follow in such situations. No time for rhetoric and statistics. I saw Omar. I saw the guns. I saw the pivotal moment unfolding in front of me, like the dramatic climax of a play. In that moment, I was no different than the people I help. I had to make a choice —the best one I could. I had a wife at home. I had a little girl. I made a choice and hoped it would work out. I hoped the consequences, the ripples, would be good.

"No, wait!" I yelled, leaping from my SUV onto the unusually crowded side street. "I know this man! I'm Dr. Steve Valle. I need to talk to him. Please let me have a chance to talk to him."

It was a long shot, pardon the pun. It wasn't really my place to interfere. I wasn't even sure whom I was talking to. The universe maybe. I hoped someone was listening. I also knew that as soon as I stepped out of the car, I was stepping into the potential line of fire. But there just wasn't time to worry about that. I had to mentally block that part out.

"Omar, it's me, over here. Look at me!" I waved wildly.

I can only imagine what I looked like to the tense group of officers. They gazed at me, bewildered, frustrated. They were taken aback and clearly not happy about my intrusion on their turf. And that's fair. A civilian busting into the middle of a standoff can get people killed. I was in the way. An unwelcome presence.

Guns were steadily drawn and aimed. All I could envision, as I kept my focus on Omar, was the young cop I saw out of the corner of my left eye collecting a trophy by popping the big Black dude, and me getting shot in the process.

"Get back! Get out of the way!" he yelled. Others echoed his sentiment.

I did so, and shouted back, "He's not armed. I'm a doctor, and I can talk to him. Please give me a chance." Or something of that nature. I prayed they would hear me.

My voice hung in the silence.

What seemed like eons later, I heard a commander yell out, "Hold your fire! Let him try."

I proceeded across the pavement and right up to Omar, aware of the guns, aware of the weight of what would come next. Omar's eyes were glazed over with fear and rage. I looked him straight in the eye.

He didn't blink. He was in a daze.

I waved my hands in front of his face. "It's me, Omar. It's Doc. I'm here. Look at me. Tell the cops it's okay and you have no weapons. Do it now, Omar!"

Apparently he still didn't see me. He was in a daze of panic and bewildered fright. He paced back and forth across the stairs in front of me, talking gibberish, as his eyes darted from me to the gun-drawn officers over my shoulder. As the cops came closer, he looked at me with what seemed to be a glimmer of clarity. I think he saw me for the first time.

I tried again: "It's going to be all right, Omar. It's going to be all right."

Omar looked at me directly. At last.

I kept my eyes focused on his eyes, hoping he would recognize my look of firm caring. It would be a familiar look to him. He had given me a lot of practice in this type of de-escalation while he was a resident at Grace House. Even so, the occasional flareups when I intervened between him and other residents were nothing like this. I found myself in an unknown territory.

"Thanks, Doc," Omar gasped. He collapsed onto the porch steps, weeping. His shirt was drenched with sweat. Exhaustion and grief and confusion took over. As he slumped to the ground, he smiled the biggest smile imaginable and wept some more. "Thank you, Doc. Thank you. They would have killed me, you know. They would have killed me, Doc."

When people leave Grace House, they leave the network of peer-run support. They are bereft of group guidance and accountability. I can no longer keep tabs on their daily choices. Outside Grace House, their risks increase exponentially. One initial slip might have nothing to do with the desire for a substance, but that slip can escalate.

Emotions tend to run high for these folks. Life's stressors take a heavy toll on them. It might be a fight with a spouse. A tussle with a boss. Just being in the world is a breath-by-breath challenge. They live on the brink. We all do, really. It is just that these guys are that much closer.

4

"Grace Always Bats Last"[13]

It's not what we've done that matters most...it's what we can become.[14]

Luke was the first president of the peer-led structure I set up at Grace House for guys who had no safe place to live after they had gone through a treatment program or been released from prison or jail. In 1997, after about a year of getting the kinks worked out of the self-governing structure, Luke approached me about an idea that was brewing in his head. "Doc, the Salvation Army Rehabilitation Program has a women's section that works well with the men's program. My heart breaks when I see the women doing well, making it through the program to graduation, but then having no place to go afterwards. I have a proposal for you to think about."

I had an idea of where he was leading me in this conversation. Luke had an incredible passion for helping others that sometimes bordered on the edge of overzealousness. He had a driving and forceful work ethic and a never-give-up attitude. At times, I had to reign in his enthusiasm, but most of the time, his exuberance and drive produced positive results. He had earned my respect, so I learned to listen to him.

He explained his proposal like this: Grace House was a duplex. We could move some of the guys around and create a separate space for women. It could work. They would have their own entrance and privacy, their own mini community. We could all come together on Sunday evenings in the living room for a joint community house meeting.

"I hear you, Luke," I said. "And I share your concern about the lack of housing resources for women. But a coed sober house? That would be pioneering. Plus, we'd need a unique and strong peer coordinator, someone with your level of skills. I don't know of any women who could fill that role."

A few months passed after this conversation. As we were ending our Sunday evening community meeting, Luke asked if I could stay a bit longer.

"What's up?" I asked.

Luke had come prepared with his solution for how the house could be arranged to accommodate a women's unit on one side of the duplex. "They'd be separated by the duplex wall. They'd have their own secure entrances, separate kitchens, and sleeping quarters. And, Doc, I've got the perfect person who could be the women's peer coordinator. Her name is Elvira, and I'd like to introduce you to her."

Breaking New Ground

Though there was a scarcity of affordable post-treatment housing options for women at the time, my professional colleagues raised some eyebrows when I mentioned the idea of a coed sober residence as one possible solution to the problem. I too was leery of the risks inherent in having males and females in early recovery living in such close proximity, without professional staff to oversee the process. Before moving forward with Luke's proposal, I met several times with the male peer community to discuss the risks and the opportunities of a coed residence. After the peer leaders and the other residents reached a consensus of approval, I forged ahead, notwithstanding the raised eyebrows of my professional peers and my own fears.

One of the protocols I established at Grace House was that potential new residents not only had to complete a written application but also had to have a face-to-face screening interview with the entire community. It was mandatory for all house residents to be present at this meeting and to vote on whether the candidate would be accepted into the house. When Elvira presented herself for the interview, it became clear to all that she was a take-charge, no-nonsense person who was serious about her recovery. It didn't take long for me and her peers to recognize her leadership ability.

Elvira told us during the interview that she came to Massachusetts because her probation officer in New Jersey mandated that she enroll in the Salvation Army's Rehabilitation Program in Saugus; otherwise, she would be sent to jail. Having been detained at Riker's Island in New York City for a short time, Elvira wanted no part of any jail. She had kicked a three-and-a-half-year heroin habit at Riker's Island, cold turkey, without any medication to ease the discomfort of withdrawal.

Elvira complied with her probation officer's requirement and entered Sally's six-month program. She completed it successfully. However, once she was on her own, without any accountability, she started using again. She went on a nine-month run of drug use and ended up living on the streets. She eventually admitted herself into a short detox program. Then, instead of going back to the lifestyle she was familiar with, she voluntarily entered a half-way house program. She stayed at Ryan House in Lynn, only streets away from Grace House, for two years.

Elvira explained that, while she had sobriety while at Ryan House, she still felt she needed an environment where she knew she would be safe, where she was accountable for not using, and where she would be a part of a supportive community. Several residents of Grace House who also graduated from Ryan House knew of Elvira's positive history there. They respected her. She was unanimously voted by her peers to be the first female coordinator of the female side of Grace House.

Elvira made her mark as the first female coordinator. At one Sunday meeting, she asked if the women could organize a Christmas tree decorating party and invite folks from outside the house who were in recovery to come to the house for a celebration of their being sober. "Holidays are really tough for us, Doc," she said. "Many of us have burned a lot of bridges; some can't go home. So, having a

Christmas tree here would help us get through the holiday, counting our blessings rather than feeling the loneliness, guilt, and shame of Christmases past."

Elvira and the other women in that early coed group started a tradition of holiday gatherings at Grace House that lasted twenty years. My daughter Marissa contributed to it by baking brownies. These celebrations expanded my concept of family, which took on new meaning as I realized the Grace House community had become family.

Elvira would likely never have made it to Grace House if not for a probation officer who knew how to use the leverage of jail time as motivation for probationers. Elvira shared with me and others at Grace House that her probation officer knew her neighborhood in the Bronx and Harlem was filled with risks. The lifestyle she had fallen into—continuous drug use, drug-seeking behavior, negative peer associations, and accompanying criminal activity—would eventually result in her being reincarcerated. She knew, as did her probation officer, that she needed to be admitted into a treatment program, and that she would resist if left to her own devices. They had discussed the option of transferring her probation to Massachusetts before, but this time, she had no option besides Sally's if she wanted to avoid incarceration. It was her last chance to break the cycle of drug misuse, arrest, confinement, release, rearrest, and incarceration.

I never met Elvira's probation officer, but I did have several conversations with him about her progress at Grace House. I consider him and many other professionals like him to be champions of much-needed justice system reformation. Such leaders have the courage and the vision to think outside the box and to be creative and innovative as they walk the tightrope of protecting public safety and simultaneously trying to help others change the course of their lives. These frontline probation and parole officers and their supervisors are vital soldiers battling in the trenches of helping to break the cycle of addiction and crime.

Conceptualizing an Effective Residential Treatment Program

In the early 1990s, after about fifteen years of developing, overseeing, and consulting with other healthcare and criminal justice organizations around the country regarding programs for individuals with alcoholism, other drug addictions, and co-occurring mental health disorders and trauma, it struck me that many very good programs fell short in one critical area: providing the necessary housing support and accountability people in early recovery need to sustain the progress they made while in a treatment program. I found this was provided for people leaving community healthcare settings but glaringly absent for people with an addiction problem who were released from prison or jail.

Though I kept active in the behavioral healthcare and rehabilitation treatment world throughout my career, my focus gradually shifted toward working with public safety organizations (e.g., law enforcement, jails, and prisons), the courts, and individuals involved in the justice system's community supervision departments of probation and parole board. As the managed care approach of insurance companies began to cut the length of time an individual was granted to remain in treatment programs and covered by their health plan, I witnessed an erosion in the effectiveness of treatment. Individuals needed more than five to seven inpatient days to address their problems meaningfully. This amount of time barely allowed the individual to medically stabilize. It was not treatment. As this trend became prevalent in the 1980s, I was drawn to the correctional treatment field, where programs of much longer duration could potentially be offered.

The two crucial elements—I felt then and still do—that need to be present for the recovery process to get started are (1) time away from use of alcohol or drugs for the body and mind to stabilize and (2) a safe and structured housing environment after initial completion of a first stay in a treatment program.

Jails and prisons provide these two elements better than do healthcare-based treatment programs. Correctional programs are better at addressing the chronic disease management issues of people with addictions because they are not subject to the limitations imposed by insurance companies. In contrast, in the healthcare-based treatment world, services are driven by insurance companies' approval of coverage for the acute phase of addiction. Focusing exclusively on what is only the starting point of recovery is shortsighted. It's a Band-Aid approach that does not allow people with addiction to begin addressing their core issues. The brain, impaired by chronic addiction, needs time to heal and repair. Cutting the coverage for time spent in treatment is more costly over the long run and does a great disservice to those afflicted with addiction as well as others who are affected (e.g., families, employers, and others in the person's circle).

In 1985, my consulting company, Valle Management Associates, received a first-of-its-kind contract from the Massachusetts Department of Correction to develop and operate a correctional treatment program for multiple drunk driving and other substance abuse offenders. The program was situated in the minimum-security Longwood Treatment Facility, located in the Bostonian neighborhood of Jamaica Plain. Based on an evaluation by the Department of Correction's Research Division, the Longwood Program proved to be a successful pioneering model for treating hard-core drunk driving offenders and those with other substance use disorders. My company designed and provided the treatment services, while the Department of Correction provided the housing, security, food, medical, and other operational services.

I operated the company out of the apartment in my North Common Street home, which a decade later became Grace House.

Dr. Dennis Humphrey was the associate commissioner and director of program services for the Massachusetts Department of Corrections at the time. One day, we were talking, and he said something like, "Well, Steve, you've developed a really good program for chronic drunk driving offenders, but these men in medium security are not like the drunk driving offenders you've worked with at Longwood. Do you think you could do the same for a higher level of security inmates—men with significant histories of criminality in addition to their serious and chronic alcohol and/or drug problems?"

Dennis explained that the Department of Correction had a large population of inmates with alcohol and other drug problems who kept reoffending and returning to the system. He expressed the department's view that their crimes were mostly driven by their addiction. Though the department provided some basic drug and alcohol education, he was a strong advocate for creating a unit solely dedicated to an intense treatment program. He felt that an immersed housing unit could address not only their alcohol and drug problems but also their propensity for criminal behavior. He asked if I could develop such a model program.

I accepted the challenge. The Department of Corrections then awarded my company a second contract to develop prison-based programs in two medium-security prisons for inmates with chronic alcohol and other drug problems. At that time, there had never been a substance abuse treatment unit for medium-security inmates in the Massachusetts prison system.

I knew that the justice-system-involved person had many complex and unique needs, beyond what I was used to treating in the healthcare arena and the Longwood minimum-security program for drunk drivers. These inmates' addictions had spiraled down so badly that criminal activity and repeat involvement in the justice system had become a way of life. They were addicted to a criminal lifestyle, mindset, and behaviors, as well as to alcohol and drugs. I realized that traditional alcoholism and drug abuse rehabilitation approaches would not work well with those experiencing multiple co-occurring problems (e.g., mental health, criminality, trauma, and other stress-related disorders) in addition to having substance use disorder(s).

I asked myself, other professionals, friends, and colleagues involved in peer recovery programs what might work with this population. From these conversations and meetings, I formulated a new model to help criminal offenders recover and change their lives. I felt strongly that we had to reset the intervention and treatment system dial. Instead of a rehabilitation approach, which was in vogue in the behavioral healthcare field, what was needed with this population was a *habilitation* approach. We needed to focus on teaching the skills for adaptive living these individuals had never acquired. Because their alcohol and addiction to other drugs often began at an early age (the preteen and teenage years), their normal cognitive, emotional, and behavioral development was delayed or had been stopped dead in its tracks. Though most of these individuals were in adult bodies, emotionally and cognitively they were stuck in preadolescent or adolescent stages of development. Our new model needed to account for this delayed emotional development and the assault on the executive functions of the brain.

I was grateful for my master's and doctoral training at Penn State and Boston University. My studies afforded me the experience of working with people who had a variety of physical, social, and mental disabilities. I had grasped the critical value of helping people by focusing on developing their strengths not on emphasizing their shortcomings. Instead of relying on their old skills, emotional responses, and thinking styles, they needed to learn (many for the first time) the thinking, emotional, behavioral, and social coping skills that would allow them to get back what alcohol and drugs had taken from them.

This perspective crystalized when I visited the Delancey Street Foundation in San Francisco and met with its pioneer founder, Dr. Mimi Silbert. Like myself, Mimi did not share the same background as the residents of Delancey Street, yet she had a vision, drive, and passion for helping people who were living on the streets, had prison/jail backgrounds, and were severely addicted to alcohol and/or drugs. She pursued her vision tenaciously and built an organization and programs that transformed lives. These were the same kinds of lives for which I was now challenged to provide a program in the Massachusetts Department of Correction.

Mimi Silbert and her colleagues developed an internationally renowned rehabilitation program using peers as the primary agents of change. I was captivated by what I witnessed at Delancey Street. Their therapeutic community approach greatly influenced the eventual development of my behavioral change model. We shared a similar core belief that "the people who are the problem can, themselves, become the solution."[15] The seeds for Grace House were fertilized in my mind during the inspiring and invaluable conversations I had with Mimi. Could a similar approach work in a home setting, without a program and staff to guide the residents? It would be a small home, not a traditional program run by a professional staff, but totally self-run by the residents.

Could it support itself financially? Would the politicians and public policy folks allow for such an experiment in resocialization? Would the neighbors?

Three Critical Factors for Success

From my experience in the Massachusetts Department of Correction and later in programs in Texas, Florida, Maryland, Pennsylvania, and other states where I was providing consulting and technical assistance, I learned that treatment can be extremely effective in correctional settings. Program services offered in these settings are valuable tools for inmate management and resources that can reduce recidivism. Working with offenders who were sentenced or held awaiting trial for a significant amount of time, I identified three critical factors that were lacking in most community-based treatment programs but present in jail/prison programs: (1) mandatory and monitored time away from the drug; (2) the leverage inherent in the criminal justice system to enforce consequences in order to influence one's choices; and (3) a structure that controls and organizes one's daily contacts and movement.

By recognizing these three simple but powerful factors, we were able to build the type of program services needed in correctional settings. They became the foundation for Grace House and my treatment model, which I called Accountability Training, to help individuals attain the tools necessary for achieving sustainable recovery and changes in the way they viewed themselves and the way they acted toward others.

Mandatory and Monitored Time Away From the Drug

Ryan, a former Grace House resident, said to me as I was giving him a lift to the train station near Boston, "I hated being in jail, Doc, but it saved my life." In fact, justice settings provide valuable time away from access to alcohol and/or drugs. There is no substitute for the value of time away from the drug.

In recovery, it is essential to allow the brain time to heal and restore its cognitive processes so one can think clearly and make rational choices. The executive functions of the brain are impaired under the influence of alcohol and/or drugs. This is one explanation for the frequent relapses that occur for many when they leave the safety of a detoxification and short-term treatment program in the community. There simply is not sufficient time in most behavioral health programs for the brain to heal. Sufficient brain healing does not happen in "spin dry" detoxification and short-term rehabilitation programs. For treatment to be successful, participants need at least four to twelve months away from addictive substances. I think one of the reasons Delancey Street programs are so successful is that Mimi Silbert had the wisdom to require a two-year commitment from program participants.

Time away from the drug also allows participants to better face the core developmental and psychological issues that got neglected in the process of addiction, co-occurring mental health disorders, and trauma. The program needs to not only address co-occurring mental health disorders but also provide trauma-informed care. Without sufficient time, it is not realistic to expect participants to deal with such core issues, and if their core issues are not addressed, their vulnerability for falling out of remission and into a relapsing condition significantly increases.

Addressing the core issues underlying the addiction process involves working on learning how to reframe one's thinking, beliefs, and consequent behaviors. Thus, the emphasis of our programs inside jails/prisons and of our community supervision or diversion programs is to challenge the participants about their faulty thinking patterns and to teach them how to formulate new thinking patterns they can apply upon release from custody or supervision. This takes practice. There are no shortcuts to the process. Repetition, practice, and constant rehearsal are necessary for mastering the skills of thinking differently. Participants must learn these skills, in addition to acquiring basic information about addiction, trauma, and co-occurring mental health disorders.

In justice-system settings, insurance companies cannot interfere with time away from the drug by dictating to staff that a person must leave treatment due to insurance limitations. Nor can participants in a correction or court program sabotage their own recovery by checking out against medical advice (AMA) because they feel better after completing the detoxification phase, as is often the case in voluntary, community-based treatment programs. In some cases, people are sentenced to jail with the condition that they participate in a treatment program. In other cases, they are incarcerated in a pre-trial housing setting while waiting to appear before a judge. If the jail has treatment services in the pre-trial housing unit, the inmate may have the opportunity to volunteer to participate. In either case, they will not leave the institution any time soon.

"So, if you're going to do the time, why not do part of it in a program that may help you get your life back?" Our staff were trained to pose this question at new men's or women's groups or at orientation meetings with inmates. They explained, "There are fewer fights and disruptions on a treatment program unit, and staff are trained to help you address your issues. But we realize it also takes guts to step away from the regular prison/jail culture. You're going to get hassled by other inmates, and the reality is, treatment is hard work. You'll work harder on the treatment unit than elsewhere in the jail because you will be working on you. But you won't be alone in this change journey. You'll have the help of staff, and more significantly, the help of your peers."

This message was driven home for me in one of the many informal conversations I had with Ryan while he was living at Grace House after being released from his two-year jail sentence. He said, "I'd done a lot of programs, Doc, but they only scratched the surface of stuff I had to work on. But in jail, I had the time to face my fears. I don't think I'd be alive if it weren't for the programs in jail. That gave me time to get my head screwed back on straight."

Ryan got his barber license while in jail and supported himself in his early years at Grace House by cutting residents' hair for a little or no fee. A few months after being released from jail, he got his first paid job at a nearby barber shop. He has over twelve years of sobriety at the time of this writing. Lately, he has supported himself and his young daughter by driving for Uber and has been a peer support and model for people who come to Grace House. Ryan's road to long-term recovery started in jail, where he had sufficient time away from any use of alcohol or drugs. His time of incarceration allowed his brain to heal, while providing him with safe housing, the support of caseworkers and counselors, and the opportunity to learn a new skill he could translate into a job upon release.

The Leverage of Authority Figures

The second factor justice-system programs have that other programs do not have is the authority to sway individuals to consider other lifestyle options rather than simply continue a repetitive pattern of substance use and criminality. These programs can incentivize a person to comply with the demands of the treatment program by offering a reduced sentence or less restrictive conditions for probation or parole upon release. The consequences of not following a judge's or probation/parole officer's supervision plan can be significant. This gives justice professionals a degree of power over the individual's immediate future that does not exist elsewhere. Thus, leverage is a critical factor in motivating individuals to begin and remain engaged in the recovery and change process.

I learned how powerful leveraging a position of authority for good can be by sitting in Judge Al Kramer's courtroom and by having many discussions with him and Chief Probation Officer Andy Klein in the judge's private chambers. Judge Kramer was fervent and persuasive in his conviction that drunk driving offenders are usually not social drinkers but rather problem drinkers who need more than education about the dangers of drinking and driving. He felt such people are best served by being mandated to attend both professionally operated treatment sessions and peer-run Alcoholics Anonymous (AA) meetings. He felt they would not voluntarily do so without being coerced by the court. In Judge Kramer's courtroom, if an operating under the influence (OUI) offender missed any meetings, they were returned to court to appear before him or another judge, with the prospect of jail time hanging over their heads. He called this strategy of nudging people toward more socially acceptable behavior when they would not likely do so on their own *tourniquet sentencing*.[16]

At the time, this was an unheard-of approach for treating first-time offenders arrested for driving under the influence. The state had a mandatory educational program for first-time OUI offenders. However, chronic drunk drivers drive under the influence multiple times—some studies[17] say dozens of times—before they get caught and have to appear in court. Judge Kramer asserted this more than once in a passionate, compelling voice as I sat in his chamber, along with Andy Klein and the court clerk. Judge Kramer believed alcoholism and addictions could not be treated effectively with education alone. People with alcoholism and addictions needed to be immersed in intensive treatment and be held accountable to demonstrate they were no longer drinking. His position was that chronic alcohol offenders needed to be drug tested, attend AA meetings several times a week, and complete the educational groups required of them by regulation. Their attendance required verification by their peers. Judge Kramer identified this as a condition of their probation: "It's your choice to comply, or you can go to jail and have some time to think about it."

The art of tourniquet sentencing was not left behind when Judge Kramer left the bench in Quincy. I continued to use it in the correctional and court-based programs I ran and in my training programs. My company at the time (Valle Associates/Right Turn, Inc.) partnered with the Quincy District Court to carve out a new model for treating justice-involved people with alcohol/drug problems. It did what Judge Kramer insisted be done with drunk driving offenders, even those arrested for the first time: immersion in intensive treatment that held them accountable for not using alcohol or drugs and for attending three to four AA meetings a week. Judge Kramer worked with local AA groups to have trusted members sign off on attendance cards attesting to an individual's attendance, including that they had remained for the entire meeting. Judge Kramer and Andy Klein met with the leadership of local groups to make sure this would not conflict with the voluntariness of AA meetings. This was revolutionary at the time and controversial.

Not all AA chapters agreed to this approach, but over time it had become the norm. It worked so well that it became the model for creatively involving the courts with the self-help resources available to help a person in their journey of learning to be alcohol and drug free. If the person could not do so, there were consequences. The consequences, however, were designed to gradually increase the leverage of the court to incentivize the individual to comply, not as a punishment but as an affirmation.

We wanted to give the message "Okay, we see you. We see the struggle. We see the pain. You are breaking the law and that isn't okay, but we want to help with the why." I smile looking back at this. It is said there's a line between treatment people and corrections people. The huggers and the sluggers. And there *is* a line. I've spent a career lifetime working to bridge that gap. However, I couldn't have started down such a path without innovative pioneers, such as Judge Kramer and Andy Klein, who saw the bigger picture. We were a natural match: we believed many could, and would, recover from their disease if given support, a community where they could find encouragement and others would hold them accountable for their moment-by-moment choices to use or not use alcohol or drugs and get behind the wheel of a car.

I once had a private conversation with Walker, an inmate at the Essex County Jail and House of Correction, that illustrated the leverage principle I learned from Judge Kramer. The conversation was at the end of a peer-run community meeting.

"Doc," Walker said, "if left to my own devices, I'd be out of here and do my time in another pod. Done that dozens of times before. But this time, I've got no choice but to stay if I want to get the judge off my back and get out sooner." He explained that the system took his choice away, but then he backtracked on that: "No, really, I did that to myself. I know I've got to do the time one way or another. This time I want to make it stick, Doc."

Walker explained he wanted the judge to know he had completed the treatment program that was stipulated as one condition of his sentence. "I want to get on with my life when I'm released, Doc," he told me.

Walker successfully completed the treatment program at the jail and was released. Because of his long-term recovery and modeling of sustainable recovery and change, which began over ten years earlier, when he was discharged from the Middleton House of Correction, Walker now runs his own successful global Internet business and is involved in helping others. He also volunteers his time and talents for a nonprofit organization I founded over twenty years ago to help individual residents of Grace House and others in their recovery and change journey.

Structure

It can be a shock to participants in a justice-involved treatment program to find themselves not in control of their everyday movements and choices. The peer associates they hang with, where they go for social engagements, what they do outside of their work—all are now subject to a structure that is imposed upon by authority figures.

A person's life in active addiction is chaotic. It is driven by unpredictability, emotional instability, and impulsivity. Having structure and structured activities can bring order to that chaos. Participants in criminal justice programs are held accountable for following a wide range of structures they likely would not follow on their own. These include making one's bed daily, placing one's shoes in the same place every night, arranging one's clothes, being on time for meetings, reporting to the probation/parole officer at a scheduled time. The predictability of structure brings a sense of relief and has a calming effect when one's life has been so out of control in the world of using and drug-seeking behavior. Structure is a precursor to feeling secure and safe in one's environment. It provides a sense of control when one's life is mostly out of control.

One of the many lessons I learned from Pat was that ex-cons (his preferred term to refer to himself and other released inmates) actually respect authority figures when they impose structure and expect compliance with the rules, as well as when they call them on their behavior, as long as it is done fairly and the guys perceive it as coming from a genuine sense of caring for them as individuals. If they feel respected, even when the hammer is about to come down on them, they can accept the consequences of their bad choices. Of course, they may not let those in positions of power know it in the moment. "I did the crime, Doc. If I get caught, got to do the time. That's just being a man, Doc," Pat said to me many times.

The life of crime Pat was once immersed in was a chapter he had closed and moved on from. Instead of taking from others, he had become a giver and caretaker. He helped scores of men establish a foundation of recovery time at Grace House. He kept high standards requiring no use of any alcohol or drugs and no violence of any form. He also made it clear to residents that they were expected to follow a structured set of rules about such things as visitor hours, who was allowed to visit residents, decorum, and doing chores at Grace House. Because he did so with caring and empathy, the residents followed his rules and the example he set. The structure he imposed was respected because it limited the kind of interpersonal drama that often happens when a strict structure is missing. I never had to worry about stability at the house when Pat was in charge. We were on the same page, and the other residents knew it. If guys had mental health issues, Pat was very protective, provided they did their part by not using drugs or alcohol and staying out of trouble. That was not always the case with Mikey.

"Doc, it's Mikey again," I recall Pat telling me. "You know the kid that was just scooped up and put in the jail on a domestic charge? He's been at the house about six months, and I know for a fact he didn't do the crime he was charged with, because I was with him at the house the exact time his girl said the event occurred. I told his lawyer that, but because of his record, the judge put Mikey behind bars awaiting trial. He won't last long in there, Doc. He'll be a target for predators because he's too fragile with his mental issues. The gangs will be all over him to be a runner. He has no resources to hold off the pressure. I told his lawyer we'd take him back at the house because he hasn't been drinking here and he was sober when he got arrested." Mickey was the type of resident who needed to be held to a strict structure to be able to stay out of trouble. The same was true for Alex, Jimmy Nine Lives, and others. Pat took these guys under his wings and kept a close eye on them. They responded to his tough love.

We had a norm at Grace House that residents had to have completed a treatment program in either jail/prison or the community before they could be considered for acceptance. Because Grace House did not have any professional staff, we felt it important for individuals to have demonstrated the desire not to use drugs or alcohol by completing a treatment program. Being a resident of Grace House required a high level of motivation and the capacity to be independent—to adhere to the structures provided for daily living. Grace House offered residents the opportunity to transition out of the security of a treatment program where staff provided structure, before being entirely on their own. Once they were at Grace House, they had to follow the established rules and structure. It wouldn't come from a professional—whether that be a judge, probation/parole officer, professional caregiver, case manager, administrator, or other authority figure they were comfortable with or whom they could con—hovering over them to remind them what to think and how to behave. Instead, they were accountable to their peers, to those who walked in their shoes.

"You can't con another con, Doc. We see the game when it's being played, because we played it; it's what we did to survive. They know we will pull their card. They live by the rules and structures of the house, or they move out," Pat said many times in his raspy, no-nonsense voice —both to me and to the residents at weekly community meetings.

When I set out to establish Grace House, I felt I had to create a mechanism through which everyone bought into the success or failure of the house community. For me, instituting this structure meant letting go of a lot of the controls I normally had when developing or overseeing a program. I was used to operating with professional staff present to direct day-to-day operations. One of the protocols I established for Grace House involved the admission process. I determined early on that the decision about who could become a resident of Grace House should be made by the community. I would be a filter, if necessary, but it was their collective decision. Prior to the Sunday evening community meeting, we held a house meeting at which anyone desiring to become a resident was interviewed by the whole peer community. This was the structure we used for initial acceptance as well as for re-acceptance if someone relapsed.

In Mikey's case—and in others from time to time—the community voted to waive the six-month program completion requirement because the circumstances warranted it. The other residents knew Mikey from the time he spent at the house prior to his arrest. Though he had relapsed, Pat, as the house president, felt the community was strong enough to take him back. In such instances, the house president checked with me if it was okay. In my twenty years as the "rational authority" and trustee of Grace House, I never had to question the community's judgment in accepting a resident, either initially or for readmission. Relying on the consensus of peers and the strength of the bond created by the resident community, I learned, was a better diagnostic tool than the formal professional tools I used in programs to assess readiness for change and appropriateness for admission to a professionally run program. Peer pressure, harnessed for good, is a powerful dynamic for growth and change.

I witnessed Pat doing this for dozens of guys over the years. Residents always knew the Grace House community (and particularly Pat) had their backs. The one caveat was they could not be involved in any criminal behavior. If they slipped and started drinking or using drugs, they could not stay at the house. We would see to it that they got the help they needed, if they wanted it. Pat and others who had cars often drove former residents, as well as current ones who had slipped and started using drugs or drinking again, to detox programs. Pat and I wanted them to know we believed in them and they had a safe place to go to when they were ready. Pat and the peers at Grace House could be counted on in a jam.

Mikey had a chronic drinking problem and co-occurring mental health disorders. He was supported by his monthly disability check because his illness prevented him from holding a steady job. He maintained sobriety for periods of time but struggled with repeat relapses. This time, because his girlfriend filed a domestic abuse charge, he was not released to the community under probationary supervision but was sent to jail to await trial. After being found not guilty months later, he came back to the house and maintained sobriety for about eight months. But after another argument with his girlfriend, who had taken him back, he again picked up a drink. No one saw this coming; he was doing well, grateful to be at Grace House and have Pat mentor him every day. Yet, instead of picking up his cell phone and calling one of his peers for help, he picked up a drink. He was unable to control the obsession and compulsion to continue drinking. Picking up that first drink led to a downward spiral of compulsive drinking. Mikey, like most individuals with alcoholism, had a broken stop button. Once he started, his drinking got out of control.

One evening, he sauntered into the house and tried to go to his room unnoticed, hoping to sleep off his latest slip, but Joey, his roommate, came to Pat and told him what was going on.

I had stopped by the house to get my suitcase on the way to the airport to catch a flight and was in an adjacent room, so I overheard the conversation between Pat and Mikey.

"Mikey, why the hell didn't you call me or one of the guys?" yelled Pat. "You know we'd be there for you. You know the rules of the house. You can't have used and stay at the house. The safety of the house comes first, so you can't stay here under the influence. You didn't do a crime, so that's good. It would have been better if you didn't try to hide it from us, but it is what it is. You dance, you pay the fiddler," I heard Pat say. "But we'll get you into a detox. You do the program again, and we'll take it from there. It's your choice, buddy. Bite the bullet and start again."

In the early years of Grace House, I sometimes had to step in if I was on the premises or I got a call from whomever was president asking me to come by and give some backing to whatever decision had been made by the house leadership. But after the first several years, the ethic of the house had become second nature to the community of residents, so I was rarely called upon. The peer leadership had earned my confidence that they would make decisions in the interest of the overall good of the community. I had learned to let go of trying to control and instead trust in the peer group process.

"Are you going to cave or take that step, Mikey? You know we've got your back," I heard Pat say emphatically.

In another setting, it would be unlikely for a resident, like Joey, to call out a peer, especially when it was a matter of losing one's bed or status in the treatment community, jail, or community house. One of the cardinal rules of the offender culture is not to rat on another. At Grace House, however, guys learn that when someone has a slip, peer accountability is not a gotcha moment but rather a means to keep them from having a full-blown relapse. Everyone has a responsibility to the house and other residents.

"The greater good of the community takes precedence over the individual" is a mantra that was heard over and over from Pat and me, or whoever was president of Grace House at the time. It is a code of Grace House. Residents know they have to accept the consequences if they don't follow the structures that have been set up for everyone's benefit and instead engage in unwise behaviors that put themselves, the reputation of the house, and others at risk. They also know we will get them the help they need, if they chose to ask for it.

From Chains to Change

5

INSIDE GRACE HOUSE

Before anyone was accepted into Grace House, they had to appear before the whole community of residents to explain why they should be approved by the peer group. They also had to agree to abide by all the rules of the community. The residents voted on whether to accept someone, and for acceptance, the vote had to be unanimous. The community was responsible to make sure the new residents understood the rules of the house, which we referred to as cardinal, major, and house rules. Key among the cardinal rules were zero tolerance for any use of alcohol or illegal drugs, no violence or threats of violence, and no criminal activity. Accountability to each other, the house peer leaders, myself as the "rational authority," and the community guided the day-to-day operations of Grace House.

Essentially, I challenged residents to rebuild their lives by living life on life's terms—with support and accountability, growing spiritually and in community with others, first in the house and then in the larger community. We had no brochures or marketing literature, staff, grants, contracts, or taxpayer dollars to rely on. We had no Internet at the time. People found their way to the house by word of mouth from the network of ex-cons and the recovery community in the area.

Paying the Rent

The residents sustained Grace House largely by the rent they contributed from whatever jobs they could muster up.

Early on, I asked if anyone in the group had experience with finances or managing a budget. Danny immediately spoke up and volunteered to be the house treasurer.

I was reluctant at first to turn over to the residents the collection of rent and the responsibility for paying the bills. However, Danny had confidence in his ability to do so and explained that he did this regularly in his business. Most of the residents at Grace House had problems with the misuse and abuse of drugs and alcohol combined, but Danny's primary drug of choice was alcohol. He didn't have any criminal history, unlike most of his peers at Grace House. He prided himself in being a successful businessman when he wasn't drinking and had come to Grace House because he needed a safe place to get sober —a place where alcohol was not available and people around him were not drinking. Loneliness and the lack of accountability inherent with living alone were his downfall. Danny was one of the first residents to use the word *accountability* when referring to what he needed to do to maintain consistent sobriety.

The weekly rent was deposited in a lock box to which only he and the president had access. By choice, I did not have a key to the box. I felt it was important for the residents to know I trusted them to be responsible and to be honest with each other.

The finances were managed by the peer leadership. Danny, as treasurer, had primary responsibility for monitoring the collection of rent each week. He deposited the checks into the Grace House checking account and made sure the bills were paid. At the community meeting, he gave the weekly treasurer's report and let the others know who was falling behind in their rent. Although this sometimes resulted in tense moments, the individual who was late or falling behind in their rent inevitably accepted the feedback from Danny, because it came from a peer.

The house-generated funds were never enough to carry the house financially, so I stepped in each year to cover the inevitable shortfall. At the end of the day, it was more important to me that the residents learn basic money-management skills—such as paying one's rent on time, and experiencing the effect on others when they fell short—than that we always have a healthy balance sheet.

"Keep Coming"

I modeled my approach for creating a social culture within the house after the modified therapeutic community model that is well respected in the correctional treatment field.[18] But with no staff on site to direct the residents, as was the case in the prison- or jail-based modified therapeutic community, I only taught them the basics of the approach. Then I put it on them to be accountable to the integrity of the house mission and to each other. They could consult with me and look to me for support, for guidance, and to mediate the disputes and conflicts that inevitably arose. Most of the residents were savvy in the street and prison culture code of conduct. I emphasized that, if they wanted to hold onto a job in mainstream society, they needed to develop more adaptive ways of getting along, instead of relying on the power and intimidation tactics that were common ways of relating in jail. This was no easy feat to accomplish. But the vernacular they were accustomed to, such as using the F-bomb in conversations, wasn't going to cut it in most workplace settings. I explained all this during our Sunday evening community meetings in the living room of Grace House.

In the early years, I regularly sat in on the Sunday evening community meetings, teaching and coaching the residents on how to run their own meetings. In time, as the peer community became its own watch dog, I became just an observer of the process. The power of peers policing and holding each other accountable was far more of an influence than I or other professionals could ever be.

What I found interesting was how much residents looked forward to my coming on Sunday evenings. They were open to my challenging them with corrective suggestions that they say or do something differently to create better outcomes and better lifestyles. I challenged them to practice changes in behavior with each other and then demonstrate those changes to me. "Practice with each other and show me next week how it's working or if it's not working for you," I often told them. I suggested they act "as if"—fake it till you make it—until they felt comfortable with a changed behavior and encouraged them to look to their peers for help in changing.

The Sunday evening meeting was one of the few mandatory rituals of Grace House. It was a time for each resident to check in with the community. Over time, I came to appreciate the importance of this time set apart for group accountability and connection. Showing up for a meeting, having an open mind, and declaring one's intention is a powerful reinforcing factor in the personal change process. In fact, this reaped dividends far beyond the meeting itself. It reminded me of a message I often heard at 12-step meetings: "Keep coming."

By Sunday evening, the residents were usually spent from a week of work and a day of catching up with their kids or significant other—if they even had a weekend day off. Most of the residents had to string together several jobs just to make their rent payment; buy food; pay child support, court fees, outstanding fines from the Department of Motor Vehicles, or transportation expenses; chip away at old debts, etc. Working six and seven days a week, often at more than one job, was not out of the ordinary. Downtime was infrequent, so showing up for the Sunday night community meeting was not an easy commitment.

The issues raised and discussed and the connections made at these weekly check-ins became the glue binding the residents to one another, creating a sense of community that would carry the dynamic of the house spirit through the week. Whenever the house got out of sorts, I could inevitably trace the cause of the discord to a slacking off in weekly meeting attendance. Though not designed as such, the house meetings were more therapeutic than a lot of the therapy groups I had run or supervised as a professional.

While Sunday evening community meetings were typically a time for residents to connect with each other and with me, occasionally things got heated. When emotions ran high, the verbal volleys became intense, and residents' nonverbal language could be threatening. If this occurred in a jail or prison program, a correctional officer (CO) or other staff member would put a lid on the intensity. At Grace House, no such staff members were present. It was just me and the ten to fifteen residents gathered in the living room. These episodes occurred frequently in the beginning and became less frequent as the culture of respect grew in the house community.

Initially, I wondered if this experiment in resocialization would blow up in my face. There were a few times when it came close. At one Sunday evening community meeting, for example, Terrell lost his temper at other house members.

"Doc, I got something," he said.

I asked him what was going on. "Address your peers," I said, "not me. I don't live here. This is your house. What have you got for the community?"

And so he did that. "Whoever's putting clothes in the washer and leaving them there for hours, stop. It's not right. It's disrespectful. I wait for the guy to come down and get his clothes out, so I can get my stuff done. We all got jobs and places to go and things to get done. No one likes handling another person's wet clothes. It's not just me; others have the same complaint." Leaving clothes in the washing machine and hogging the dryer were constant infractions, and Terrell had had enough

The group sat there waiting for the culprit to own up to his stuff so we could get on with it. They wanted to go chill for a bit before starting the work week. I wanted to close out the meeting, get back to my Marblehead home, relax, and be with my family. But not tonight. It wasn't going to be a routine Grace House meeting.

"So, whoever's doing it, own it now and let's move on," Terrell said in a firm tone.

A period of silence followed. No one said anything. Terrell was getting noticeably fidgety. Others knew one of the new residents was guilty of the infraction. Normally, this would be no big deal, so I expected it to be settled quickly. Newcomers not getting into the flow of living at Grace House was a familiar issue. The offender would usually apologize to the community, and that was it.

But on this evening, no one owned up. I found out later that several community members had spoken to this resident, who was suspected of taking other people's food from the fridge without asking and repeatedly left dirty dishes in the sink for someone else to clean up. So, as is often the case, it wasn't really about the wet clothes in the dryer. It was about a series of irritants that were building tension within the house that were disrespectful. For many people, such behavior would be annoying but not a big deal. But for Terrell, it had become a big deal. Not only was it festering for him but it was bothering his girlfriend also. Letitia was a resident on the women's side of the multi-family duplex. They had met at the Salvation Army Rehabilitation Program, having both graduated from the faith-based work program. I didn't know it at the time, but Letitia had brought up the issue to Terrell several times during the week, and yet the resident had not changed his behavior. I got why it had become a big deal.

Inevitably, if a person in early recovery had a conflict involving their significant other, within or outside the house, it had the potential to become a tinderbox. Relationship issues, I came to learn, were the number one threat to a resident using again or getting involved in criminal behavior. Such issues also were a key trigger for relapse.

In Terrell's mind, his manhood was being called into question. He couldn't look weak to his girl, but even more so, he couldn't look weak before his peers. He had to do something. If an issue like this was settled on the streets, it could get ugly. But because the community was learning to be respectful of the reputation of the house, during the week, his peers had told him to let it go. "Hey, Terrell, let it go. Take it up at the Sunday meeting, when the Doc is here," Omar had said to him.

Terrell had big-time anger management issues. He had a calm and happy-go-lucky disposition on the outside most of the time, but when he felt dissed, it didn't take much for him to lose it and get violent. He had spent many days in the segregation unit due to fights and threats of violence at the New Jersey prison where he did time before coming to the Sally's.

"So, Terrell, is this a house pull-up for everyone, or do you have something to say to someone?" I asked.

"Nah, not worth it, Doc. He knows who the fuck it is. Just be respectful of others and take your own clothes out of the washer and put them on the table, okay? There are other people living here."

There was a long silence hovering in the living room, like a huge water balloon suspended in mid-air that was ready to burst from the volume of water it was attempting to contain.

Then Terrell lost it. "I'm fucking sick and tired of going downstairs and finding the same set of clothes sitting in the washer, hogging the machine so I can't do my clothes. It's fucking disrespectful. What the fuck! Come on, man. What the fuck!"

Dead silence.

Terrell got up and postured toward Dave, the most recent new resident, chest out, fists clenched at his side.

"Terrell, it's okay. Can you please sit down? It's not how we do things at Grace House," I said, hoping my request didn't set his anger off even more. "I would really appreciate it."

Terrell looked around the room, paused, looked at me, and took his seat.

"Thank you," I said. "Here's the deal. Let's table this for now. The person who is doing the deed has one opportunity to come up to me at the end of the meeting and talk this over. Then we'll meet with the peer leaders and find a solution. If you take this opportunity and own up, the only consequence will be an apology to the house at next week's meeting. If you blow it off, there will be other consequences I'd rather not discuss right now. It's up to you. At Grace House, it's not about punishment, it's about owning your stuff and being accountable to your peer community."

The offender did come up to me after the meeting and apologized to the peer leaders. I spoke with Terrell, and he was okay with it.

He apologized to me for losing it. "But, Doc," he said, "I put a lid on it before it got bad. I did okay, didn't I? If this was on the streets or in the big house instead of Grace House, it would have been settled with my fists. I'd end up in segregation for weeks. I know it's not the way to go. I'm trying, Doc."

I told him he did good. "Thank you for showing me respect and putting a lid on it. That wasn't easy for you to do, I know. Thanks for showing respect for Grace House. We don't need the cops here breaking up a fight, do we? This house depends on you and everyone to make believers out of all the naysayers. You're doing just that. You've made a believer out of me. Time to chill and get some sleep. I'll check in with you tomorrow. Love you, bro."

"Love you too, Doc. And thanks. I'm learning."

Terrell smiled and gave me a hug.

A Typical Sunday Meeting

"Let's circle up, guys," the president of the house said to start each meeting.

Then we recited the serenity prayer in unison: "God, grant me the serenity to accept the things I cannot change, the courage to change the things I can, and the wisdom to know the difference."

In this way, we followed a standard format for the weekly house meeting, though each house president added their own twist. The following is the basic structure of the weekly meetings held at Grace House.

Opening ritual. This usually was a prayer or motivational saying, where the residents gathered in a circle, with arms around each other's shoulders.

Business items. Announcements were made concerning the day-to-day operations of the house.

Chore report. The chore coordinator gave a report on each person's detail assignment for the week.

Rent/house finances report. The money coming in and going out to maintain the house in good working order was reviewed by the treasurer. Residents gave an account to the community of any rent issues they might be facing.

Individual check-ins. This was the meat of the meeting. Each resident reported on how they were doing physically, mentally, emotionally, and spiritually, at the moment and during the prior week. They reported to the house community how they were working on their individual recovery plan and if they were having any issues. Were they attending their mutual support meetings? Were they taking their medications as prescribed? Were they going to their counseling sessions, complying with drug tests or other probation/court requirements, and moving forward on their spiritual path? During this check-in period, issues around relationships, frustrations or tensions with other residents, and stressors eating at them and potentially threatening their recovery came up. If anyone needed help or some assistance this was processed as well.

Care and concerns. Residents expressed concerns about other residents or asked for help handling a matter or challenge they were facing. Sometimes they requested prayers for a loved one. Sometimes they called out another resident on an issue that concerned other residents.

Issues or questions for further discussion. Usually this item was passed over quickly.

Closing circle. Residents again gathered in a circle, with arms around each other's shoulders, and were led in a motivational thought, a similar prayer to that which was said to start the meeting, and/or a moment of silence for other sick and suffering people with addictions.

One night, just before the closing circle and during the issues and question section, I heard a nervous but determined voice from the corner of the room.

"I got a question I've been wanting to ask the Doc," said Fitzy, looking at Pat for a nod of approval. Fitzy was a new resident at the time and knew the code of respecting the hierarchy of leadership. He had a great smile; engaging personality; and a bold, confident air about him. I had seen Fitzy on Marblehead Neck that week. He told me he was doing some carpentry work at a neighbor's home, then he sped off in his pick-up truck, loaded with tools and ladders. Mr. Reliable, another resident at Grace House, was also in the truck with him.

Mr. Reliable had become my most dependable chauffeur to and from the airport for the scores of trips I had to take for business. I'd rather pay him than an unknown taxi driver, and it gave us a chance to connect.

His prison record prohibited him from getting a job as a taxi or limo driver, yet there was no one more trustworthy. For this reason, although his real name was Jim, I gave him the nickname Mr. Reliable.

When Fitzy spoke up at the community meeting that night, you could have heard a snowflake drop from the wintery storm that was brewing outside. Silence and blank stares by the other guys followed his voice. A few nervously squirmed in their chairs. Pat looked at me, ready to pounce if Fitzy showed any iota of disrespect.

"Why are you doing this, Doc? I mean, this was your home! You could be with your family in Marblehead tonight, but here you are with us. You show up during the week now and then, and you're always taking calls from us. Why, Doc? Why Grace House?"

"Thanks for asking, Fitzy. I've been asked this question from time to time. It's a question I'm sure many residents have wanted to ask me, and several of my colleagues and friends have. It's a good question, Fitzy," I said. "Bottom line for me, it's a calling. You couldn't pay me enough to be here as part of a job or obligation. But it's not a job or an obligation for me. I can only explain it as a spiritual calling to do my part in helping others who are hurting. But it's not about me really, Fitzy. It's about you and the other guys in this room—those who have come before you and those still out there looking for a refuge; a safe shelter from the storms of alcoholism, drug addiction, trauma, and criminal behavior; a chance to start anew. Something inside my being, my spirit, led me to provide the vehicle of this house I once lived in with my family to be a potential transport toward recovery and transformational change. For me, the calling is a spiritual thing. I can't explain it logically or rationally. But I did know enough from my background, from reading the Good Book and from *Alcoholics Anonymous* (the "Big Book"), as well as from the people who influenced me in my life, that I couldn't ignore the calling. But it's up to you and your peers to make it work. I wouldn't be here if I didn't believe in you, in everyone in this living room, and the hundreds who have sat in your seats. Neither I nor any of you would be here if other people hadn't been there for me in my time of need to support, to help, to correct with caring and accountability, and to believe in me. So Grace House is one way of me doing my part, of giving back, of passing it on. And I ask that you in turn do your part. Respect yourself; respect the others in this house, who now are your family; and pass it on to the next person who is in pain and in need of a helping hand. Give back to get back, as they say in the halls, right, Fitzy?"

"Yeah, you got it right, Doc."

There was a pause and then Fitzy softly murmured, "Thank you, Doc."

Silence filled the room, and then, one by one I heard, "Thanks, Doc," emanating from the circle of fifteen men, from twenty-four to sixty years of age. The sincerity and gratitude that flowed from the looks and the few words spoken that evening were grabbing. It was one of the most memorable moments for me at Grace House.

After canvasing the room, looking each person in the eyes, I nodded a humble "thank you" back. "Okay, guys, it's been a long meeting. Who's going to take us out?" I inquired. "Pat?"

"Circle up, guys," Pat said as each person stood and put their arms on the shoulders of those beside them. Then he led the group in the closing prayer: "God, grant me the serenity to accept the things I cannot change, the courage to change the things I can, and the wisdom to know the difference."

Perhaps it is the divine within that calls us to consider others. Perhaps it is what many (particularly those in 12-step programs) refer to as their higher power, or God, moving them toward internal change. Perhaps it is the God of our particular faith or religious belief. Or unbelief. Perhaps it is the power of our group, the good orderly direction (GOD) we find in community with others. Whoever or whatever that force or higher power or spirit is, we must ultimately answer or surrender to that One to break free from the cycle of addiction and co-occurring mental health disorders. The answer and the calling is beyond each of us, and it is beyond me.

The White House Visits Grace House

For released inmates and other justice-involved individuals (e.g., those who were experiencing homelessness, the mentally ill, and those who had completed a residential rehabilitation treatment program), the length of time spent at Grace House varied. There was no minimum required length of stay. Many initially intended to stay for a short time, perhaps a couple of weeks, and then move on to another housing situation, but most ended up staying several months. Some stayed for as many as three to ten years. The culture of Grace House fluctuated, depending on the residents' rate of turnover. When residents stayed for longer periods of time, the climate of the house was significantly more positive.

This longevity of the residents was a huge benefit to the stability of the house. It facilitated the emergence of a strong peer leadership that fostered the identity of Grace House as a place for people who were serious about maintaining long-term recovery and changing their lives. In so doing, the reputation of Grace House grew exponentially.

Even though I had prevailed over the threat by the Lynn City Council to block the house from opening as a housing alternative for unrelated individuals in recovery, I purposefully kept a low profile and avoided any publicity. That all changed after a phone call from President Obama's Office of National Drug Control Policy informing me that its director, Michael Botticelli, was going to be in Massachusetts and was interested in visiting Grace House sometime in early August. An advance team of security agents would be coming unannounced, prior to the drug czar's visit, to conduct a surveillance and security review of the house and its surroundings.

As I was leaving the Middleton House of Correction a few weeks later, on my way to meet Pat at Grace House, my phone rang.

"Doc, you sitting down?"

"I'm in the car, just leaving the jail. What's up, Pat?"

"We're doing our chores, and out of the blue, I hear a knock on the door. I open it and after a brief hello, bingo! There are suddenly three gorillas in suits going through the house. No warning. No heads-up calls. They just appeared. They're checking everything: exits, entrances, rooms, basement, doors, windows, attic, everything. It's crazy, man! We used to run from these goons and now we embrace them. I guess that White House guy really is coming?"

To get a personal visit from the White House drug czar to honor the courage and resiliency of the residents in their daily battle with addiction was a big deal to the residents. And to me. I had served on the board of directors of the New England Institute on Addiction Studies (NEIAS) with Michael Botticelli for several years. When he received the offer to join President Obama's White House staff, he gave me a call and asked if he could meet with me and Christine Cole, another NEIAS board member, over a cup of coffee or lunch to chat about his upcoming appointment. He had known of my nomination to be director of the Substance Abuse and Mental Health Services Administration in President Clinton's second term and thought I might have a perspective that would help him transition into the White House staff. Michael, Christine, and I met in Cambridge over a sandwich, shared our excitement, and tossed around thoughts about how he could make a unique contribution to the addiction recovery field. Christine and I assured him we'd be there to support him and remind him never to forget his humble roots, no matter how successful he became.

It was a full house packed into the living room of Grace House on that memorable afternoon of August 8, 2014. Michael had brought with him a contingent of aides, security personnel, and a reporter from the

Washington Post. Sheriff Frank G. Cousins Jr. and some of his key personnel from the Essex County Sheriff's Department were huddled in the room, along with the residents, some of whom were former inmates under his department's jurisdiction. Protocol notwithstanding, Sheriff Cousins would do whatever he could to support another person's recovery, even if it flew in the face of acceptable norms and protocols.

Michael connected immediately with the guys. He talked about his personal battle with addiction and how he got to a place where his life was spiraling out of control —just like many of those who were listening to him. Yet here he was now, on the White House staff. His addiction didn't stop him from achieving the seemingly impossible. He described how hard it was to crawl back from his abyss and have a meaningful life of recovery. He did so by doing the hard work of recovery, one day at a time, and by building a community of support, giving back to others, and being involved in service. He spoke with candor and humility, and inspired all of us to not let our addiction define us but rather to embrace a recovery lifestyle filled with unlimited possibilities, quality relationships, and service.

His message was an epic story of hope and resiliency that left us all smiling, tearing up, and hugging each other. At the end of his comments, he called on Pat to stand up and receive a gift of gratitude from President Obama. He presented Pat with a White House pen set that acknowledged Pat's volunteer service, which had saved and lifted up so many lives at Grace House.

Michael and his staff stayed for another hour, mingling with the residents, making sure to speak with every resident who wanted to do so. My eyes filled with tears of joy as I saw the rays of hope shining in residents' eyes. *Grace*, I thought, *is amazing*. I couldn't have scripted it more perfectly.

As the limos were pulling away from the house, Pat, Mr. Reliable, Sheriff Cousins, and I stood where the chalk mark of a dead body had been drawn a few years before. We waved goodbye to Michael and his staff and looked at each other. We all had smiles.

"That was pretty amazing, eh?" Mr. Reliable piped up. "He really loved when I showed him my tattoo, Doc."

"That was a presidential visit!" Sheriff Cousins said. "It's time to tell the story, Steve, so others can learn from Grace House's success."

Little did I know, back when I was responding to the calling within me to abandon my effort to sell my home and instead give it to those who had no home, that it would one day be recognized by the White House's Office of National Drug Control Policy.

From Chains to Change

6

PASSING THROUGH THE TRAP

After passing through the initial security checkpoint of the Middleton House of Correction and entering my personal security code and fingerprint in the automatic fingerprint identification system (AFIS), I waited along with several other uniformed and non-uniformed staff at the entrance to the trap. The officer in the glass-encased central control room engaged the switch controlling the sally port door. Then I was inside the pedestrian trap—the passageway all visitors and staff must pass through to access the jail (inmates and supplies enter through a separate secured trap area). The thunderous clank of the motorized steel door clamping shut behind me, with its cold, lifeless form, reminded me—as it did all who take these steps—that once you cross into the trap, you have entered a new world, a world unlike any other. Whether you are an inmate, a visitor, or staff, the lens through which you view life will never be quite the same.

This was the first of many security check points scattered throughout the jail. Whether it's your first time or (in the case of career correctional professionals) your hundredth or thousandth time, the trap is a vivid reminder of a constant that does not change: you are no longer in control of your life. You are subject to the authority of others. You are accountable to an authority greater than yourself. When in the trap, like it or not, your reality has changed. Whether it be for a short visit (eight to twelve hours a day) or for months and years, there is a commonality of experience that can't be denied. If you've had this experience, you and I are linked. We are connected because we share a common bond of human experience that is distasteful; frightful; intimidating; and yes, hopeful—all at the same time. We may never talk to each other about it, but we are connected nonetheless. We are a community forged by our ambitions, mistakes, passions, joys, sorrows, hopes, and dreams for one another and for our world. We are a community of millions, larger than many states and some countries.

Such is the world of a person with addiction serving time because of a crime related to their behavioral health condition. Such is the world of the family and loved ones of those caught up in a web of seemingly unending addiction and imprisonment, whether it be the physical prison of walls and barbed-wired fences or the emotional prison of shame, guilt, and remorse. And such is the world of the corrections, treatment, and social policy professionals who have made a choice to embark on a career of helping others so our society can be safer and remain free.

Because we pass through the trap of this human condition and connection, whether by choice or circumstance, we are a community. And because we are a community, we are accountable to each other. The offender with addiction is accountable, as are their family and loved ones, professionals, and all of us. Each day that I pass through the initial security screening area of a jail or prison and line up to enter the trap, I recognize I am now surrendering some of my freedoms to forces and authorities over which I have no control. Most prominent among these are my freedom of movement and my freedom of speech. I must submit to background checks and security clearances. My person and possessions are subject to being searched for contraband: drugs; weapons; objects, such as paper clips or spiral bindings of a notebook that could be made into shanks or weapons; cell phones; pens; etc. You cannot go through the trap without giving an account of yourself to others. In this way, passing through the trap within a prison can be seen as a metaphor for the addiction and recovery process.

In addition, my personal safety has been turned over to others. I've surrendered to the men and women in uniform, all unarmed, most of whom I only know by title (captain, lieutenant, officer) or by referring to them as "sir" or "ma'am." The normal control over my personal space and belongings is also now surrendered to the authority of others. My movement is restricted by boundaries determined by someone in authority.

I consciously made a choice to cross the threshold of those steel doors separating bondage from freedom to convey a message of hope and change to inmates whose freedom to make such a choice was forfeited by making one bad choice: to use alcohol or take drugs. This is a choice a person with addiction—especially if involved in the justice system—cannot make in seclusion. For an alcoholic or other drug-addicted person, once that first choice to use alcohol and/or drugs again has been made, all bets regarding their next series of choices are off. Their thinking, emotions, decisions, and behaviors are unpredictable because they have surrendered control over their cognitive capabilities, emotional regulation, and social connections to the unpredictability of the drug(s). They have crossed over the threshold and into the trap of active addiction, where control of their life is forfeited to the chemicals they have become dependent upon. Addiction has taken their brain hostage. Inevitably, that first bad choice to pick up and use drugs again results in criminal behaviors for which there are numerous negative consequences—the loss of personal freedom, dignity, and respect being foremost.

Once in the trap, one thing is quickly apparent. I can't get through it without receiving assistance from another. I need the assistance of my peers to engage the switch that releases the door to the trap so I can move forward. Similarly, we can't get through the entrapment of addiction without the help of others, especially one's peers.

I am not alone in this temporary entrapment. I'm part of a community of others who daily walk through the trap, and no one can go it alone.

An Introductory TRAC Training

The behavioral change model I created is the recognition that a person with a substance use disorder, co-occurring mental health, and /or trauma disorder needs the help of others (most notably their community of peers) to recover from their addiction and to change criminal behavior. We all (e.g., cops, correctional officers, professional caregivers, academicians, laborers, tradesmen and women, neighbors, managers, administrators, people in faith communities) do better when we use the enormous resources of support found in our community of peers. I'm always surprised at the visceral tightness my body feels when those imposing and cold steel doors close behind me, even after thirty-plus years of going in and out of prisons and jails. I often wonder if the correctional officers, managers, teachers, support staff, and other professionals I worked with as an outside contractor ever became numb to the chill and finality of passing through the trap. After all, these dedicated career correctional professionals, for whom I've learned to have an incredible level of respect, did not have the opportunity to be an occasional visitor, like me, given my status as a contract worker. Yes, we worked side by side, but that is not the same as being a correction professional. This is their career. This is their job. Passing through the trap is an everyday, several-times-a-day occurrence.

In a correctional facility, prison, or jail, one's ID is the first line of security, and attention to this little detail matters. This is not unlike what has occurred in our society since 9/11, where IDs have co-opted personal recognition and even relationships. You may be known and trusted, but if you don't have the proper ID, you don't get to pass any further. Attention to such detail in a jail or prison is a critical element of security and must be respected, no matter your title, position, role, or rank. Each time I entered the trap, I needed to do a quick attitude check on myself. That served me well on this particular day at the Middleton correctional facility, as it got me in a better frame of mind for the reason I was there: to address the eighty men housed in the addictions treatment cell block called TRAC (Treatment for Recovery and Change in Corrections) and to do a training with the staff and inmate peer-group leaders.

I wasn't quite sure what I was going to say to the audience of inmates and staff, but the mental gymnastics I was indulging in because I had to give an account of myself to the authority behind the glass-enclosed control room hit a chord. Personal change starts with accountability. Being aware that we are accountable to authority is a necessary first step in the change process. It is a concept I intuitively resist, but nonetheless accept as reality when I want to accomplish a goal that involves the cooperation of others—which, in this case, it did. I would much rather walk right through the trap on my own terms and timeframe than be subjected to checks, searches, and questions. But the reality is that if I want to accomplish what I want to do, it requires complying with the demands of others. Inmates and staff alike quickly learn this lesson: respecting the authority of others is a requirement for survival in prison or jail…and in life.

As the officer nodded her head, signaling that my compliance by repositioning my ID in a more visible place was acceptable, I noticed her engaging the control that released the steel door of the trap, thus opening the entranceway to the next security checkpoint.

Before entering the interior grounds of the facility that housed, fed, and provided program services to the inmates, and where all movement was under continuous surveillance by cameras and officers (some with K9 dogs, some without), I approached a locked chain-link gate. This gate was part of a fifteen-foot-high chain-link fence topped with a huge coil of barbed wire. There could be no further movement into the interior buildings of the facility until a loud clang was heard, indicating the officer inside the control room had electronically released the gate. I was outside now, and it was raining. No matter. The lock would be released when central control was ready and able to do so—cold and rain notwithstanding. My position, my title, my standing in the greater community didn't matter at all. The officer with the hand on the controls determined what was safe, and only what she determined mattered at that moment.

One could wait for quite a while if a lockdown was in progress or an incident had occurred. Those of us who stood in the rain waiting for the gate lock to be released had no idea if we would be there for fifteen seconds or fifteen minutes. Our movement was under the control of the officer to whom I had shown my ID. She could see us, as we were on camera, but we were no longer able to see her or gauge what was going on. Knowing someone is watching you yet not being able to make contact with them in any way feels unsettling. The people waiting with me at this checkpoint could only stay put, be patient, and get wet.

Still waiting and getting wetter, I remembered to use one of the tools that is taught in the program at the jail and that is core to all 12-step-based recovery meetings. I recited the serenity prayer to myself: "God grant me the serenity to accept the things I cannot change, the courage to change the things I can, and the wisdom to know the difference."

The eyes of the coworkers who had passed through the trap with me and were now awaiting clearance to pass through the second security gate met mine. We half smiled at each other, with an understanding look that signaled our collective acceptance of what we could not control and our shared hope that this time the wait would not be too long. *Of all days to be caught outside*, I thought, *it had to be one of those bitterly damp and cold New England days!*

One of the subtle but quick lessons to be learned in corrections is that other people's agendas need to be regarded, sometimes above one's own interests. The greater good of the group taking precedent over the preferences of the individual is a core principle of my Accountability Training change model. It is a principle of change that applies to inmates and staff alike. I planned to convey this vital message to the inmates: to grasp sustainable recovery and change, it is necessary to change one's thinking from "me" to "we." I would also teach this principle to staff, as an essential paradigm for functioning as a team and for the program to be effective. I've always taught my staff as well as professionals from many disciplines that the most effective programs are those wherein staff model the principle of "we before me" (the first step of the AA 12-steps begins with "we").

Accountability to your community of peers is a core principle to be grasped by staff and program participants alike. "Showing respect for your colleagues is critical if you want to be effective in your job of helping inmates change.

As you do so, you will receive respect in return" is a mantra I frequently cite when instructing treatment staff who work in jails and prisons. Being accountable for doing your part is showing respect for the community of peers whom you work alongside of each day.

I heard the loud click, signaling that the officer in central control had unlocked the door. I pushed my hand against the cold, wet fence, ever mindful of the sign clamped to the chain-link steel that read "Do Not Slam Door!"

We all darted through the open courtyard, crouching to keep the cold rain from pelting our faces, and opened the next door, which led to several office areas and to the next security door. I was alone at this door and only had to wait a few seconds, as the officer with the keys at his post in the booking area noticed me waiting. He reached for his door key ring, and with his hands protected by plastic gloves, opened the last secure door. I walked through it, then entered the corridor that led to the open courtyard that hosted several inmate housing units and about a thousand inmates.

Correctional officers are good at what they do: keeping staff and inmates safe under very harsh and demanding circumstances. "Because they do their job, we can do our job of giving inmates the tools to recover and change—if they choose to do so," I have repeated numerous times to civilian staff working in correctional settings. Officers are expected to do more with less. And they're not the only ones. When a librarian's job in the jail gets cut, other staff must cover the area, as the availability of a library is crucial to maintaining morale, motivation, and order. When part-time staff members are laid off, their duties must be picked up by full-time staff who are already overburdened. Similarly, counselors, educators, healthcare workers, managers, and administrators all have to do more with less, due to budgetary limitations throughout corrections departments in all jurisdictions.

As I walked into the courtyard connecting the various housing units of Middleton House of Correction, my thoughts were solidifying what I would say to the eighty inmates and staff awaiting my arrival. Little did I know at the time, but the new officer at central control had triggered a mental lesson plan for me.

The way out of the trap of addiction and criminality for the offender and into a lifestyle of recovery and change is by following a model of change involving principles of accountability, respect, and community. The fact that my Accountability Training model for change evolved from listening to and observing offenders in prisons and jails from around the country and not from the textbooks or from my educational training is for me a humble reminder that, in real life, the students are often the teachers.

The talk I gave that morning went something like this:

"Good morning, guys. Welcome to TRAC. I'd like to talk to you about the Accountability Training model for recovery and change that you will be participating in and shaping over the next few months. I'll give you some background into what the TRAC program is all about and the accountability model that anchors what we do, so you can decide for yourself if you want to buy in. It's okay if you choose not to, but for the next twenty minutes or so,

I'd appreciate if you'd give me the respect of listening to what I have to say before you decide.

"After that, it will be up to you if you want to participate or go to another unit. The TRAC program, in a nutshell, is about change. Participating in programs is no joke—they take a lot of work, so it's important that you are invested in the process. TRAC is not about just doing your time. You can do that in the other units of the facility. It is about making the choice to fully engage and do the hard work of changing your life so you don't come back here again. The key point to remember is that you're not alone in this challenge. The staff will be a resource for information and a tool to help you and hold your feet to the fire in a supportive manner. The community itself, made up of your peers, will also be a significant part of your change process. But ultimately, it's you who will be doing the work of change, if you want to make the choice to do so. TRAC is about choices and change. If you want to change the trajectory of your life, it can happen here in TRAC. It takes courage to go against the jailhouse culture and build a community of respect. But that is exactly what being here in TRAC is all about: building a community based on respect. It's up to you to make the choice, take the risk, and engage yourself in a process of real and meaningful change. Fair enough?"

After surveying the sea of expressions and eyeballs staring back at me, I sensed they were saying, "Yeah, whatever. Got nothing better to do, Doc, so go ahead."

I continued, "First, it's important to know that the origins of the model applied here in TRAC were not found in some textbook or college course. The model evolved over time by listening to guys in prison and jail programs—guys just like you, who had the courage and character to make a strong statement to their peers. They were 'sick and tired of being sick and tired' and were going to step up to the plate, take some risks, and be committed to recovery and change. The model evolved from the input and feedback of your brothers, wearing jumpsuits just like yours, in jails and prisons in several states around the country. It is also from what I learned by coaching, and at one point living with, others with addiction issues at Grace House in Lynn, many of whom had traded their jumpsuits for jeans, shirts, and ties.

"The Accountability Training model we use here in TRAC is peer driven but staff directed. Professional staff are in charge and have important roles, but whether anything of real value happens on this unit will depend upon you. You have a choice to make. Do you want this unit to be different from other pods in the facility?

"Second, the roots of this model were nurtured in the meeting halls and fellowship of AA. The power of example set by recovering individuals who stay sober one day at a time, working hard, supporting one another, holding each other accountable, and give back by helping others, is irreplaceable. You don't get that kind of life-transforming change out of a textbook. It is found in the real-life modeling of others who have suffered from the brain disease of addiction, co-occurring mental health disorders, and trauma; committed many criminal offenses in the throes of their addictive lifestyles; and now live life free from the chains of addiction and the wreckage of their past. For offenders, therapeutic community programs—most notably, the Delancey Street Foundation in San Francisco and prison-based therapeutic communities I was involved with in Texas, New York, Florida, and Massachusetts—were all instrumental to the emergence of the Accountability Training change model."

I spent the next half hour going over the philosophy, core principles, and program components. I had their attention, I thought, but then I felt a change in the energy in the room. Guys started fidgeting, looking around, and giving those god-awful blank stares that every teacher or group leader dreads. They were back in their inmate mode: being compliant but unengaged. They were mentally detached from the moment and drifting to wherever their minds took them to help them get through another group meeting.

I stopped dead in mid-sentence.

In the ensuing silence, my mind had its own wrestling match. *What should I do now? Do I fall back to safe mode and assert my authority? Do I call on the correctional officer, draw on one of the cards of power we as staff hold: chastisement, sarcasm, nonverbal staring? Or do I just blurt out, "Class over"?* The latter would be the power-trip response of dismissal, a harsh punishment that does not even give the person an opportunity to have their say, thereby diminishing that person and conveying that they have no value. The stripping away of one's voice is the ultimate slap in the face, the ultimate disrespect card that is experienced so often by offenders trapped in the maze of the criminal justice system. It should never be used. I knew better than to pull that card. The program would be dead in the water if I did. I was at a tipping point with the group. The next few words or gestures would be pivotal.

The silence was broken by Walker, the first peer coordinator for the TRAC program, who knew exactly what was going down. "Doc, excuse me, this stuff is really good, but would it be okay if we, the peer group leaders, took a stab at it and worked on it over the weekend with others in the community who want to give their input? Kind of put our twist on it?"

I scanned the watchful eyes of the inmates, and the uh-oh look on the faces of my staff, who were wondering what the fallout would be for Walker, who had just taken a big risk in front of his peers, other staff, and the correction officers at the back of the room. All were wondering what my response to inmate Walker would be. The silence was deafening. The eyes stared at me, piercing.

Walker had clearly heard my message. He was respectfully challenging me to let the peer leaders put into practice what I was attempting to convey. I was hearing him as well. "Go on, Walker," I replied.

"Doc is saying that we are the most powerful agents of change. This program is not about the professionals, it is about what we are going to do with the opportunity in front of us here in TRAC. So, Doc, how about the peer leaders meet over the weekend and take what you've been saying and put it into our language?"

Walker was a sharp cookie, a savvy veteran of the Massachusetts jail system, having been incarcerated many times—all for nonviolent, quality-of-life crimes, entirely because of his addiction. He was rescuing me from myself and the comfort zone I was drifting into when I get into my professional tone. At the same time, he was reinforcing his leadership with his peer group: he was the alpha dog for the lower eighty-bed unit. Most importantly, though, he was buying into the program.

"You're on, Walker," I said. "That's a great idea. Work on it over the weekend with the peer leaders, and we'll go over it next week."

Wow, I thought to myself. *Yet another lesson, taught to me by an inmate. The student has become the teacher once again.* The lesson for me was that the power of recovery and transformational change lies in the peer group, if we can only listen long enough to give it voice.

Over the weekend, Walker and the peer leaders reworded some of the core principles and beliefs of the Accountability Training change model. They presented it to staff, using their own language to express the core principles from an inmate perspective. The following are the core beliefs they connected with and that had meaning to them:

- Addiction is a disease of the brain that affects behavior. It is a chronic, progressive, relapse-prone disease.
- There is no known cure for addiction, but recovery is attainable with help from others and accountability to others.
- I can change, but I need the help of a peer group to keep me in the TRAC program and to keep me on track. Change involves adjustments in one's thinking, choices, and values.

- Addiction is a disease of isolation. Recovery is a process of reconnecting with others. Establishing connectedness with one's community of peers, mentors, family, and significant others is key for recovery management.

Though many years have gone by since this rendering of the model's core principles was drafted by TRAC's first peer-leader group on the steel picnic table positioned in the back corner of the lower eighty-bed unit at the Middleton House of Correction, this reiteration has remained one of the best-received PowerPoint slides I use when I teach the Accountability Training change model. I have used it at local, statewide, national, and international forums, including when I addressed Parliament's House of Lords Drug Use Sub-Committee in London. It is my way of giving voice and a platform to the untapped potential that exists in the offender population. If we can pause, listen, and view these human beings not from the rearview mirror that keeps them trapped in the past but from the front windshield of possibility, where we can fix our eyes on seeing what potentially lies ahead for each person engaged in the change process, we will be on the road to transformational change.

Winning Buy-In

A few weeks after my introductory motivational talk to the eighty inmates, challenging them to become a part of the change process for themselves, I walked onto the unit and into Harry's office. Harry was the program director for the TRAC program at the Middleton correctional facility. Up to this point, my daily conversations with Harry had indicated that the therapeutic community program was developing smoothly.

"There was an incident over the weekend, Doc," Harry stated. "You know, one of those basketball elbows that occur during rec time."

This incident was after we'd had several constructive meetings with the peer leaders, training them in the basics of the Accountability Training model. The twelve peer leaders, of which Walker was one of the two coordinators, were starting to believe in themselves. They had hope in their eyes again. Few things are more exciting and motivating than to see in the eyes of those who have lost hope the glimmer of new expectation. They were psyched for what could happen for themselves and for the unit. As a professional, one lives for these moments, which unfortunately come all too infrequently.

"What went down?" I inquired.

"Walker took one for the unit. He's got a black eye. We don't know if there will be a community meeting at all, but he's up there. We're not sure how it will go, but the officers are on notice. Doc, I'm glad you're here."

"I'll hang out on the side of the room, Harry, and step in if you give me the nod. Let's see how the community handles it. It will be a good barometer on the health of the therapeutic community."

My staff and the officers waited with anxious anticipation as the peer leaders took their place in front of the community. I scanned the room and noticed the officers and program staff were strategically positioned in the room, ready to respond if any intervention by staff was necessary. They knew what had gone down over the weekend and were on high alert.

The staff didn't know all the details of the incident. We rarely do in such instances. But they knew Walker had been challenged by one of the jailhouse gang guys for being a suck-up to "the cops." In this case, that meant not only the officers but any of the staff trying to create a change in the jail culture. Though no one would admit it, all knew a fight went down. No one had ratted to the officers or staff about what had happened. "Just an elbow going up for a rebound" was all anyone got out of the inmates, but everyone knew Walker was targeted because he was the peer leader working with the staff. If he folded, the aggressor knew all too well, the unit would fail, and it would go back to being just another jail block where gang mentality and inmate rules of survivability were in charge. In such an atmosphere, fear, not respect, ruled. If Walker went to the staff about the assault, if he asked for protection for himself, the unit would be sacrificed. It all hinged on what Walker did Monday morning when Harry and the staff were back. Would he back down from the leadership role and cave into the strong-arm jail mentality that got played out over the weekend?

The eighty men in TRAC gathered for their community meeting.

Walker kicked off the meeting. "Good morning, community. I'm Walker and I'm a drug addict."

The community meeting went on without a hitch, as if nothing had happened over the weekend. Walker made a statement to his peers that he was totally buying into the program and that TRAC was taking the Accountability Training therapeutic community program seriously. It was a tipping point for the program and for Walker.

After Walker closed the meeting by leading the unit in the serenity prayer, I sauntered over to him. The rest of the inmates were putting back chairs and hurrying about, getting ready for the next meeting on their schedule. "Hey, Walker, good meeting today," I said with a coy but proud smile on my face. "And nice decoration on your eye, there. Did you at least make the basket?"

He smiled back. "Yeah, Doc, we scored."

Despite the attempt at derailment by the jailhouse culture, TRAC stayed on track. Walker had scored a big one for the community. He had earned the respect of his peers and of the staff. He had earned the right to lead. TRAC was succeeding not because of anything the staff had done but because of what Walker, as a peer leader, had done. His actions made a statement to everyone else: he was going to respect himself and respect what the therapeutic community was attempting to do. He wanted a chance to change, and he would do whatever it took to have that chance.

For the next several months, while Walker was in place as the peer group leader, the program had a huge impact on the entire jail. Recovery and transformational change became embedded into the jail culture, and the positive impact permeated throughout the institution. This time around, changing his life mattered to Walker, and he was proving it.

7

UBUNTU: I AM BECAUSE WE ARE

When we are finally willing to meet "what is" and stop insisting on our own version of life, real change and transformation become possible.[19]

I consider Accountability Training and how it is integrated into one's life as a modern expression of the timeless Southern African philosophy of Ubuntu. Bishop Desmond Tutu explained Ubuntu when he wrote, "My humanity is caught up, is inextricably bound up, in yours."[20] Both Ubuntu and Accountability Training are grounded in the belief that humans are relational in nature. As William Paul Young observed, "We are designed to be relational beings."[21] They both represent a similar philosophy and way of life. Richard Rohr says we practice Ubuntu "when we connect with other people and share a sense of humanity; when we listen deeply and experience an emotional bond; when we treat ourselves and other people with the dignity they deserve."[22]

Ubuntu is another way of expressing what I saw occurring in the lives of so many individuals in the Accountability Training programs in prisons, jails, courts, community corrections, and healthcare settings that my colleagues and I were involved in throughout the United States. For a span of time covering more than three decades, participants in Accountability Training programs learned how to experience sustainable recovery and transformational change by integrating its core values and fundamental principles into their lives and their significant relationships.

The New Law of Three for Recovery and Transformational Change

In establishing the conceptual framework for the Accountability Training programs to operate in a variety of settings, I began to realize that those who are successful in the recovery and change process have three fundamental things in common.

First, once they learn to be accountable for their actions and own or take personal responsibility for their choices, they cease to blame other people, places, or things for their harmful decisions. They "man up," as Pat often said to other residents of Grace House.

Second, the successful ones are able to break through the isolation, guilt, shame, and self-blaming that often accompany the addiction process and form a community of support among their peers. As I learned from inmate Walker in the TRAC program, "Addiction is a disease of isolation; recovery is a process of reconnecting with others." Discovering the support, encouragement, and power of examples found in one's community of peers strengthens an individual so they never give up. It helps them to keep working on staying sober and not using drugs—one day at a time and, critically, knowing they're never alone. We are all connected.

Thirdly, the "winners" who establish long-term recovery and experience transformational change expect to be treated with respect, and in turn, they show respect to others. They are also grounded in an authentic spirituality. The changes they make in themselves are evident by how they relate to others and in their service to others. They are no longer self-absorbed people who are just about "me," but rather now have a perspective of "we."

From these once-broken and very often forgotten and rejected people, I learned a new law of three: *recovery and transformational change, sustained over time, is attainable when the three interdependent forces of accountability, community, and respect are all at play*. These laws grew out of the three critical factors (i.e., mandatory and monitored time away from the drug; the leverage inherent in the criminal justice system to enforce consequences in order to influence one's choices; and a structure that controls and organizes one's daily contacts and movement) that are lacking in most community-based treatment programs but present in jail/prison programs. Figure 1 illustrates this model.

So, does the model work?

It does. In addition to observational and anecdotal examples of the model showing that it has an impact on people's lives, it has been reviewed by independent researchers. An evaluation funded by the National Institute of Justice concluded that offenders who completed the Barnstable County House of Correction's Residential Substance Abuse Treatment (RSAT) program, which used the Accountability Training model as its foundational curriculum, showed more than a 30 percent lower rate of recidivism three years after release than did other offenders. Moreover, the study concluded that the program demonstrated a significant cost savings.[23]

Accountability

From Wall Street to Main Street, Americans are outraged over the lack of accountability shown by leaders in every area of society. Our obsession with self-interest and the narcissistic mantra of "me first," at the expense of the greater good, has made it difficult to live up to many core American values. I see accountability as prominent among these. If we want our society to live up to its stated ideals, we—much like people recovering from addictions—need to learn how to be accountable to ourselves and others, find our spiritual selves, and build communities of support and resiliency.

The focus of accountability is on identifying one's role and the consequences for others, as well as for oneself, of the choices one makes. Then one can take responsibility for those choices, knowing that whatever actions or inactions one chooses, there will be consequences. Or, in inmate language, as one offender put it succinctly to me during a class I was teaching, "*accountability* means manning up."

Being accountable involves four components: (1) having awareness; (2) understanding the choice one made; (3) owning one's role in the consequences one's choice brought about; and (4) taking meaningful, empathic action to change. No excuses, no blaming others, and no victim mentality were permitted in the Accountability Training programs I supervised or at Grace House. While participants give reasons for their choices, they don't spend time discussing the reasons or feelings associated with the behavior being addressed, as typically occurs in conventional treatment programs.

We must learn to incorporate an accountability paradigm and value into our culture. Accepting the reality that we all answer, whether we recognize it or not, to someone or something greater than ourselves is the essence of accountability. Unfortunately, it is often only through experiencing extreme pain and loss that the principle of accountability is driven home. Emotional pain and loss are often the most acute purveyors of this reality. When we experience this, the illusion that we are in control is shattered. The painful process of addiction itself; co-occurring mental health disorders and trauma; as well as the loss of freedoms that come with having to answer to the authority of a judge, employer, family members, or others in our lives drive this reality home for many. We as humans are accountable to others and to the higher good within ourselves, which calls us to be mindful of others.

Community: Connectedness to Others

According to Richard Branson, "change happens through the power of communities."[24] The sense of belonging to a community is a basic need of human beings, like the need for food, water, and a roof over our heads. Being connected to others, being a part of something, having affiliations with others are all critical for living and for living life meaningfully. Piero Ferrucci says, "Without this belonging, we would feel like nothing. It is hard, maybe impossible, to know who we are without some reference to others."[25]

But in the process of addiction and by making choices that can result in criminal behavior, the basic human need of community is shattered. Addiction separates people from their values, the people they care about and who care for them, and society. It is the ultimate bond-breaker among people, because disappointment, betrayal, shame, and loss of trust are experienced when one is in the throes of addiction. The need to keep feeding one's addiction and to be driven to any lengths to survive another day enslaves one to the bondage of the next high. It separates and isolates. The shame and guilt are overwhelming for the person with addiction. For the addicted person who also gets involved in committing crimes to support their addiction, it is soul taking. As I stated when describing the core beliefs of the Accountability Training model, "Addiction is a disease of isolation; recovery is a process of reconnecting with others."[26]

It is often said in the halls of AA meetings that "recovery is an inside job," and for most, this is so. This refers to the internal hard work we must do in the recovery process to really change. However, for many justice-involved people with addiction, trauma, and co-occurring mental health disorders, the journey of recovery begins as an outside-in proposition. This is a subtle shift in perspective but an important one. The individual's sense of self-worth is shattered. In the process of addiction and the criminal lifestyle that often accompanies drug-seeking behavior, the wreckage caused by our past is so overwhelming that guilt and shame become embedded in our sense of identity. This distorted view of self can be changed by receiving enormous affirmation from others and by doing the next right thing. In time, we start believing in ourselves again.

Shame can be defeating. But with the support of community, the process of facing and accepting our failures and shortcomings can be redemptive. With the help of community, the self-forgiveness that is necessary for healing can be achieved. The cleansing that occurs by the support of community enables us to get back up again, no matter how many times we've been knocked to the mat. The resounding encouragement of "keep coming" heard at AA meetings from the group when they acknowledge in unison someone's sobriety (even if only for a twenty-four-hour period) is powerfully restorative. It gives the once hopeless hope again.

Bill W., who was the cofounder of AA, and hundreds of thousands of others have realized that they could not stay sober solely on their own. They needed others. They needed to be in community with others. For this reason, AA often is referred to as "the fellowship." As recovery takes hold in community, the process of reconnecting with our core personhood restores our mind, redeems our soul, and transforms our life. It is the miracle of recovery and transformational change.

Respect

At some time in our socialization process, we all know what it feels like to be seen or treated for less than who we are. Even worse is to be treated as if we are not seen at all.

When we are disrespected, we feel as if we are invisible, as if we don't exist. It is a feeling that engenders insecurity, fear, doubt, and bitter resentment.

For the person with addiction and mental health and trauma issues who is also a criminal offender, this feeling of disrespect is constant, so much so that it becomes part of one's identity. It becomes lack of self-respect. The offender with addiction is labeled and treated as if they don't exist, or are a loser, and over time, they ascribe to that belief: "If everyone thinks I don't exist and treats me like a 'less than,' it must be true."

This is often expressed by participants in the groups or individual counseling sessions we conduct in our programs. The process of addiction and associated criminality fills one with endless shame, guilt, and remorse, such that a healthy sense of self is buried, if not extinguished altogether. Add to that the humiliation and indignity experienced by being incarcerated or under the court's supervision, and we have an individual in such a state of psychological despair that respect of self has vanished. When self-respect is lost, what one does and its consequences matter little to the individual, who is stuck in a state of psychological quicksand. It is a desperate and frightful state of being for the individual, and also for the safety of others.

It took me a long time as a psychologist and CEO of a company that designs and develops correctional programs for offenders with addiction problems to fully appreciate just how powerful respect is to the offender and how it supersedes even the most basic of human needs. Career correctional professionals have witnessed inmates endure extreme physical deprivation; threats and beatings; loss of food, water, and clothing; isolation; and even the risk of death because of their longing for respect. Either they felt disrespected or needed to show other inmates that they would do whatever it took to be respected. They need to feel respected by others who mattered to them at the time and to respect themselves.

What peers think of them carries disproportionate weight for offenders' thinking process, priorities, and decisions. It takes priority in the hierarchy of needs for the offender with addiction. The shame and guilt of choices made under the influence too often sever the bonds of support and love from family, valued relationships, and social connections. The peer group, even that of a gang or anti-social network, takes the place of others. Maintaining the respect of this group is core to one's sense of self and identity.

You won't find respect mentioned as the key factor to solving the dilemma of criminality in criminal justice or behavioral health textbooks. At least I never did. I learned it from observing, listening, and connecting to inmates with an addiction problem who genuinely wanted to change. They just didn't know how to go about it. Nor do many of us professionals. From them—as was the case over my forty-year career of working with offenders with substance use, trauma, and co-occurring mental health problems—I learned that respect is the most critical thing offenders and professionals must establish with each other. Respect needs to be established for an offender to even begin considering the thought of changing, let alone begin the process of building a whole new life. Mutual respect is the essential foundation to build a lifestyle that exhibits sustainable recovery and transformational change.

Mind the Gap

Over the course of my career, I have done dozens of training workshops, speaking engagements, and presentations of the Accountability Training model throughout the United States and in the United Kingdom. A particularly significant and pivotal series of presentations occurred in London in the spring of 2010. I was riding the tube, London's subway, to visit the prison drug treatment programs where I'd been invited to discuss the application of the Accountability Training model. I was in deep thought, wondering how to present the model to my British colleagues in Hemel-Hemstead prison, or the next day in Wandsworth prison, one of England's oldest facilities. The familiar admonishment "Mind the gap. Please mind the gap" bellowed over the loudspeaker. This iconoclastic reminder that I was in a different country and culture penetrated my contemplative state of mind. And something clicked. The deliberate but thoughtful voice that cautioned passengers about the gap between the platform and the train was not one of impending doom. It was a plea for awareness, a reminder of where you are, so you can step out and safely move forward. Be mindful of the gap…but keep moving forward. Whatever gap(s) we are navigating in our life or circumstances, we are better equipped to keep moving forward when we incorporate the principles of accountability, respect, and community.

I discussed how the model is applied with both staff and inmates in the States and in a variety of justice settings. In that same week, I spoke before the House of Lords All-Party Parliamentary Group on Drugs Misuse. I related the story of Grace House and how the Accountability Training model was being applied in real time. I also spoke at the United Kingdom/European Symposium on Addictive Disorders, where I was featured as one of the event's special speakers (see appendix 2).

This week-long series of meetings and events, where I was honored and respected in ways I hadn't experienced in a long time, not only was invigorating and uplifting but became pivotal in my movement through and out of depression. It was my "rounding the mark" moment, my solstice, my new arising. The recovery and transformation model I talked about and witnessed in others had taken hold of me.

8

"I'm Me Again"

As we saw in the last chapter, respect is a key aspect of the Accountability Training change model. It also is the springboard for spirituality to emerge. It is the necessary core characteristic and anchor for the other traits of spirituality.

It wasn't until after several years of interacting with the Grace House residents that I began to observe a qualitative difference between those who had accomplished some sober time and those who had been able to attain periods of long-term sobriety. The latter group had moved from the "dry drunk" disposition or "white knuckling" sobriety they obtained when they had internalized respect for themselves and others to a serene sense of acceptance of their condition. They also demonstrated a giving-back-to-others, or service-to-others, mentality, along with the other higher order traits I viewed as and termed *spirituality*.

To be clear, the changes I observed in those few who did the hard work of recovery and change didn't turn them into saints. They just became humbler, a bit kinder, and less egocentric. But they still had their flaws. It was just that they could accept those flaws, laugh about them, and move on and through their imperfections better than others.

With all this in mind, I revised the Accountability Training model by replacing respect with spirituality as the third factor. This didn't make respect any less key; if anything, it was more key because it had expanded to include more characteristics: empathy, honesty, authenticity, kindness, gratitude, humility, and service—all defining characteristics of spirituality (Figure 2).

The curriculum I used for this was developed by one of my most seasoned senior program directors, Roger Allen. Roger championed the teaching of spirituality at the Barnstable County Jail and House of Correction on Cape Cod. I share it with you as a tool to use as a guide as you explore and develop your own understanding of spirituality.[27]

While some experience a spontaneous "spiritual awakening," as was the case for Bill W. and Senator Harold Hughes, who was one of my spiritual mentors and founder of the federal legislation that created the National Institute on Alcohol Abuse and Alcoholism, for most, the spiritual awakening referred to in AA meetings is the result of hard, gut-wrenching work. Pema Chödrön could have been speaking of this work when she said, "Embarking on the spiritual journey is like getting into a very small boat and setting out on the ocean to search for unknown lands."[28]

I have been blessed on the course of my journey of recovery from clinical depression and the effects of alcoholism to have people in my life who model what it means to live a life of meaningful recovery and transformational change. From my youth throughout the course of my professional life and the years of being connected to Grace House residents to the present, I was influenced by people who modeled long-term recovery values, healthy emotional sobriety, and a serene sense of spirituality. They dramatically transformed their lives. They lived by being accountable to others day to day, in the decisions they made, and in how they related to others. Notably, they also surrounded themselves with a community of peers who kept them connected to others on whom they could lean for guidance, help, and support.

Perhaps most powerfully, I observed how, though full of human faults, character defects, and messiness in and around their own lives, they exhibited a tranquility, an acceptance of life's curveballs, and an incredible resiliency in hard times and in periods of grief and loss. They were also nonjudgmental, gracious, and kind. They carried themselves with an attitude of gratitude and humility, displayed an authentic joyfulness in the celebrations of others' happiness, and modeled an unrelenting willingness to be of help and service to others. They exhibited the characteristics of respect, empathy, authenticity, kindness, gratitude, honesty, humility, and service in their attitudes and actions. In short, they exhibited the essence and the presence of spirituality in their lives.

This was powerfully driven home to me one day by Walker, whom I hadn't seen since he shed the brown jumpsuit he wore in one of our jail programs several months earlier.

I had just finished working out at the Boston Sports Club's South End facility. People were rushing about, showering up, and getting dressed for the start of the workday on this bitter cold and wintry February morning. Leaning over to take off my flip-flops, I heard the rattle of a commercial-size heavy-duty hamper coming my way and knew instinctively I would have to shift to the left to avoid a minor bump, if not a full-blown collision. I remember wondering in that split instance if they intentionally timed the mopping in a highly populated fitness club so it coincided with peak hours when the maximum number of people were shifting, weaving, raising arms to put on deodorant, drying hair, etc. I also distinctly remember my annoyance, a reaction that though admittedly normal, was not particularly fair. After all, the maintenance person, or "environmental engineer" (the contemporary term for what I knew as the janitor in my early gym rat days) was just doing their job and doing it so my experience would be a good one.

As the industrial-sized hamper was careening toward me, I was stuck in a rut of negative thinking that sprang from my own self-centeredness, not dissimilar from the criminal thinking and false beliefs evident in an offender's thinking. Didn't the guy know I was on a schedule? Couldn't he do his cleaning at a more convenient time (for me)? This establishment just doesn't get it. They need to change! I was into blaming, finding fault, and pointing a mental finger at him. If I were a student in one of my own cognitive behavioral classes, I would have flunked.

Fortunately, I quickly became aware that my attitude and thoughts needed an adjustment. I put into practice some cognitive behavior skills that enabled me to move out of the "it's all about me" rut I was in. As soon as I did that, I recognized Walker.

We embraced each other.

Then we quickly let go of our spontaneous locker-room man hug and shook hands sheepishly.

Shaking hands to recognize the presence of another person is a symbol of respect in normal society, but in prison it's anything but normal. Shaking hands with an inmate is frowned upon and only sanctioned in a program unit or occasional one-on-one situations. Prisons have a way of diminishing one's humanity in subtle but powerful ways. Not allowing the recognition that you are noticed as a person, that you indeed exist as an individual, which is often conveyed by the common handshake, is one of those little reminders that you are "less than." You're not a person anymore; you're just another inmate. In jails and prisons, you are referred to not as Mr. or Ms. Smith but as "Inmate Smith."

"Man, am I glad to see you, Walker," I said. "You're looking great! The staff at TRAC have been wondering how you've been doing since your release."

Walker couldn't talk long as he was conscious of being on the clock and wanted to be sure he made a good impression on his new job.

"How did you get this job?" I asked.

"I told them I had a lot of good experience cleaning latrines in my last job at Middleton. Fortunately, they didn't ask much about where I was in Middleton. I think they thought it was the college. I wasn't about to correct them and say it was the jail."

"Did they run a CORI check?" I asked, referring to the criminal offender record information check.

"I didn't give them the chance to turn me down. I'm hoping that by the time they do the paperwork, I'll have proven myself. I may not be running anymore, but I haven't lost my street skills, Doc," he said, with a coy smile.

I also smiled, thinking with amazement how resourceful and resilient people with addiction can be when they direct their street smarts and criminal thinking in a positive manner.

"Got to keep cleaning. Great to see you, Doc!" he called back to me, over the rumble of the hamper weaving its way up the tile corridor of the locker room.

I purposefully delayed my exit from the club long enough to be able to catch Walker in another corner of the gym, cleaning up a new area. "Got a number, Walker?" I asked.

"Yeah, Doc. Here's my cell. Me and my girl have a place, and we're both going to meetings and making it. Give me a call, and say hi to the guys in TRAC," he said, smiling broadly as he pushed a trash can down the hallway. Then he added, "I'm me again, Doc."

Those words echoed with me. Because I was also "me again."

When I first heard Walker's hamper barreling toward me, I was acting like most of us act, thinking like most of us think most of the time. If we're even three-quarters honest with ourselves, we know that despite awareness and interdependence being prerequisites for a well-lived life, we generally don't do more than pay lip service to these ideas. Because of my self-centered thinking, I was oblivious to what Walker or others were thinking or what demands others may have been placing on him. The fuel for good old anger and resentment was stoked by my "all about me" mentality. I'm not exempt from any of this, CEO and helping professional though I am. I mean, I'm supposed to be the teacher, but there I was, in a simple, non-stressful situation in the gym, needing to hear one of my own lessons.

Because I'm fortunate to have learned some basic cognitive self-correcting skills during my socialization and educational process, I was able to shift my thinking and control any self-centered impulses that, if acted upon, could have had negative consequences. Many offenders I see in correctional settings who have an addiction problem also have a limited education and lack prosocial models who could help them change their attitudes to better accommodate the needs and interests of others. On the contrary, most had negative role models in their formative years. They didn't get the skills they needed from the streets or from their parents (many of whom had addiction and criminal records as well) or from a gang or peer group.

Thinking before you act is so contrary to the skills of a person caught in the web of addiction and survival on the streets that it is understandable why the thought of learning a totally new set of skills can feel overwhelming and foreign. It is easier for an offender to just do the time and move on than to confront their limitations and shortcomings and try to change. I have heard hundreds of times from inmates that doing regular prison or jail time is much easier than participating in a treatment program designed to challenge them to change. In fact, for many, the first time they are exposed to other ways of thinking and behaving occurs in a jail or prison educational or addiction treatment program. Being involved in such a program is hard work, risky, and emotionally challenging. That is why it is so crucial to respect inmates who have the courage to enter into a treatment program, regardless of their motivation.

One of the teachable moments we implement in Accountability Training programs is about heightening the awareness of this innately human but inescapably damaging issue of distorted thinking. Addiction holds the thinking process captive so the person can convince themselves they can and do exist on an island. Nothing matters except the self; instant gratification is the one and only goal. Part of the recovery process is to learn how to change this self-absorbed thinking and behavior, thus evicting folks from their coveted and carefully protected island. It goes further than understanding that actions have consequences. It is about recognizing the ripple effect and seeing that the little things matter. No one wants to do this, however good it may sound, and as I am consistently reminded, it is not just offenders with addiction who find the island lifestyle appealing.

In anger management classes, we teach inmates to identify the thinking, attitudes, and core beliefs they have that lead to resentments, self-destructive anger, and harmful behavioral responses. Many of the offenders in our programs—as is the case in most offender-based addiction treatment programs—have serious anger management issues as well as addiction. Many also have domestic violence charges that stem from acting out uncontrollable anger at their partner or loved one, and doing so more often than not under the influence of alcohol or drugs. For this reason, we emphasize addressing both anger management issues and addiction concurrently.

9
SOLSTICE

The *Solstice* and its crew were motoring away from its Marblehead Yacht Club mooring, the oldest (dating back to 1835) of the five revered yacht clubs on Marblehead Harbor. We sailed past the Dolphin and Boston Yacht Clubs; the Landing, a local restaurant favorite; and the Barnacle. Situated close to the mouth of Marblehead Harbor, and with a unique boating ambience, the Barnacle is my favorite fish-and-chips New England pub.

When I moved my family to Marblehead from the Lynn Commons home that became Grace House, going to the Barnacle was my first experience of connecting to the community. It felt anchoring to be greeted by name by the owner, Jake, or my favorite bartender, Jimmy, whenever I arrived. Cruising around town and visiting the local shops and restaurants usually meant a friendly encounter with someone. This was very different from what I had experienced in the bustling urban environment I grew up in, where one could visit a host of shops and restaurants anonymously. Marblehead had a refreshingly engaging and open friendliness to it that was new to me. Connecting with neighbors and friends through community, school, recreation, and church events gave me a sense of belonging, and thus security that I came to value and appreciate.

On this Wednesday afternoon, the *Solstice* motored past the Eastern and Corinthian Yacht Clubs and toward the mouth of Marblehead Harbor, which was bordered by Fort Sewell on one side and the Marblehead Lighthouse on the other. From my assigned post on the bow, where I provided guidance to the helmsman and cockpit crew, I could see the house where I lived.

As we navigated among the other boats, all waiting for the sound of the starting gun, we had the opportunity to size up the competition for the upcoming race. It was also a time to briefly catch up with each other. As we were chatting, we passed a boat in which a couple we knew were sitting. We waved to them, and they waved back. However, something seemed off. As only friends could tell, the still silence between the couple sitting opposite each other was noteworthy. The screaming silence of interpersonal tension was deafening. It permeated the midsummer salt air, overshadowing for a fleeting moment the serenity of being on the water. It was as if a thunderstorm cloud had appeared out of nowhere. I could feel the chill between the couple like a chilly breeze coming through the harbor on a fall day. Except it was 95 degrees that Wednesday.

"They hit a speed bump in their marriage," one crew member explained. "Hopefully, it will work out."

Hopefully was the operative word. So many people try but still can't make it work.

"Maybe they need to see Steve. That's his expertise!" another crew member blurted out, as all eyes turned my way. "He's the shrink."

"Yeah, that's why they call him 'the Doc,' right?"

"You guys know not to look to me for advice on relationships," I said. "I've got the 'Gone to Lunch' sign on my office door when that topic comes up." *It's one thing to be an expert; it is a whole other thing to try and fix what's broken inside yourself,* I thought. Before I could speak further, the five crewmen burst into full-belly laughter at the irony. The sound reverberated across the harbor. It was a priceless moment of connection that only comes among humans when a bond of mutual respect and trust has been established. We didn't always say much, but we could always laugh.

While these New Englander sailors knew only snippets of my life and I of theirs, we were connected. We were linked. Every time we sailed, we worked to get somewhere together. It was the kind of connection I've felt both with and among the Grace House residents. At Grace House, the specifics of each one's circumstances may have differed, but the common thread of loss, pain, and adversity connected them, as did the common goal of continuing down the road of recovery. They were a crew, and crews know how to show up for each other.

I loved those Wednesday nights of sailing races. I loved being out on the ocean. I loved the wind and the mistakes, and the lessons learned. Those nights and those men helped me move forward. They helped me move, period. I was reminded through that process why I do what I do. And just how close we all are at any point to the brink.

On the Brink of My Abyss

I had been racing with the crew of the *Solstice* for four years when my personal life ran into a series of emotional storms and headwinds. After one race that involved competing against crews from all over New England, as I was heading to our Sunday evening community meeting at Grace House, I realized I'd reached my breaking point. I rarely missed a Sunday meeting, so I went anyway, even though I was feeling numb and directionless—like I was drifting aimlessly in a fog, rudderless and with no wind in my sails.

Several things had put my life into a tailspin. I had lost a dear friend and mentor unexpectedly to cancer. I'd lost my savings as a result of a failed business venture. I'd lost my home and my marriage and my closeness with my daughter. By the grace of God, I hadn't lost my job. I not only held onto my job, but I was thriving in it despite being in a constant state of inner torment. It was my escape from the emotional pain that overwhelmed me when I was not preoccupied with work. It provided the grounding and meaning that stabilized me during the daytime hours. But when the business and distraction of work ended, the demons of darkness attacked with a ferocious vengeance.

Unknowingly, I was suffering from a serious depressive illness I was no longer able to control and keep under the convenient wrapping of denial, despite my white-knuckling attempts to do so.

I had lost the ability to sleep, dozing for brief periods of time in the early evening and periodically during the night, only to be woken by a flood of tears or sighs of despair that became uncontrollable episodes of sobbing. I'd lost my appetite; my clothes no longer fit after a loss of thirty pounds. I had little energy except for work. I'd lost interest in maintaining friendships—the reservoir of energy to maintain them was drained dry. I hadn't suddenly become antisocial; I just had no energy to engage with others. Everything was just so hard to do. I was in a constant state of shame and pain. Despite the external accolades that came from work activities, I couldn't shake a gnawing sense of failure and worthlessness. It took every ounce of energy to muster the strength to get up every day and try to appear as if nothing was wrong with me.

I was so exhausted and weary that I started wondering if I had acquired some form of immune deficiency disease —HIV/AIDS, heart disease, or a brain tumor—that would explain the searing random headaches and mental confusion. Or some form of cancer, I thought. I finally saw a series of doctors and went through bunches of lab tests to find a medical reason for my plight.

When all the medical tests turned out normal, I had to concede and surrender to the advice of friends, that I seek professional psychiatric help. I thank God for those few close friends who cared enough to confront me with caring compassion. While from most of my work and social friends I was able to hide my anguish, the symptoms were becoming noticeable to those closest to me. The pain had become unbearable. I had become a wounded helper.

I knew I had to do something. I had resisted going to therapy for a long time, and the gentle but frequent suggestions of a colleague and dear friend to do so. I resisted his nudges to consider medication as well. *I can handle it*, my mind erroneously told itself.

On that Sunday evening, as was the custom, the guys were gathered in the living room, waiting for my arrival to begin the meeting. I trudged into the grand turn-of-the-century home, with its high ceilings and craftsman molding, the noise in my head almost obscuring my ability to lead these men who needed me so.

"Doc, you, okay?" Pat asked right away. "No offense, but you look like shit. We've never seen you like this."

Do I hide or do I share? I thought. *What would I tell one of them to do in my shoes?* The answer was obvious. "I'm not really okay, Pat." Holding back tears, trying not to show weakness in front of the whole Grace House community, I softly said, "I'm a mess. It's finally all come to a head. To top off this nightmarish couple of years of curveball after curveball, I'm getting divorced. It's too much to handle all at once. I've never felt so down, so at a loss. I'm on the brink."

There was stunned silence. No one moved. No one knew what to say.

Pat broke the silence. "What the fuck, Doc!" he shouted. "Sit down. Sit down. What the fuck?"

Those were my sentiments exactly. *What the actual fuck?* I thought, *No, it can't be over.* To a flaw, I had a never-give-up mentality. You just keep going. You make it work. For better or for worse, right? But that wasn't happening now. "You guys carry on with your meeting," I said. "I'm going to skip tonight. I've got a lot to think about. I'll get a hotel room for now."

"Doc, you've been there for us for over ten years. We're here for you," said Mr. Reliable. "We've got your back. We'll move ourselves out and set up an apartment for you. Give us a couple of days, and you'll have your own place, here, with us."

They intended to make room for me. And they did. These ex-cons with troubled lives, now in recovery, made sure I was safe. I have never been more humbled and grateful than at that moment of vulnerability. I looked at Mr. Reliable, tears forming in my eyes. I knew how far he had come in allowing himself to get in touch with his feelings of sadness and hurt. And now he was reaching out to me, caring for me as a I teetered on my abyss.

They proceeded to clear out a studio apartment that two residents were sharing, moved furniture around, and created a place for me. It was adjacent to the community room but had its own entrance so I could come and go but also be connected to the community of residents if I wanted. They gave me space, and a place.

Those first several months at Grace House gave me a lot of time to think. I spent many lonely, sleepless nights ruminating over my many losses, which kept piling on. It was sheer torment. I couldn't fathom what was happening to me; I only knew I was on the brink of despair as I dwelled on everything I'd lost over the last few years.

None was more wrenching and devastating to me than the loss of my daughter's trust at age twelve.

Initially, the doctors had told us all Marissa's tests were normal. She just needed to accept that womanhood came with pain; it wasn't that bad, she would adjust. They suggested she might be stressed and using that to avoid school. Maybe she should try therapy. These were my medical colleagues, so they knew what they were doing, right? They appeared confident, arrogant even, as they moved out of her room and on to the next patient, without so much as a backward glance.

I agonized over what they were telling me and the suffering Marissa was describing. Her eyes silently begged me to believe her—my buddy, my little girl. At least at first, she had no doubt I would fix this for her, be her hero. I always had come through for her; that's what I did. But as the days and months passed, doubt crept in for her. And she was right. The chilling reality was that I didn't know what or whom to believe. To my daughter, that meant I didn't believe her. She experienced abandonment. Everything changed between us.

Although I had lost the home of my dreams on Marblehead Neck, for three years, I found an unexpected home at Grace House. Living alongside a recovering community of ex-cons with substance use and co-occurring mental health disorders, I had a new family—one that wouldn't pass judgment or have expectations of me I couldn't fulfill. With their support, I got into therapy and went to self-help meetings wherever I could find them. It didn't matter to me if it was AA, Narcotics Anonymous, ACA (Adult Children of Alcoholics/

Dysfunctional Families), or Al-Anon (12-step self-help meetings for family members). I did the 90-90 plan you hear about: ninety meetings in ninety days. After initially resisting medication to treat my symptoms, I initiated a course of medication treatment for acute anxiety and clinical depression while simultaneously receiving talk therapy.

The combination of all three pathways—immersion in attending mutual-help groups, psychotropic medication, and professional talk therapy—slowly brought me back from the abyss and to a place of healing, and I believe, transformational change. I was involved in weekly outpatient talk therapy combined with taking prescribed medications for over three years. To this date, I have been in remission from the disorders of acute anxiety and clinical depression for over a decade.

Marissa was eventually diagnosed and given a treatment plan. We had to brace ourselves for the reality that she would forever be affected by illness, even though she had narrowly escaped death and infertility. That was no small thing to ask of a fourteen-year-old. I was able at times to do things for her, such as storming into the principal's office after the school dared send home a truancy letter. And flying her to Marco Island to sit on the balcony so she could recover from surgery with sun and breakfast buffets.

Throughout those years, Marissa's mother was more there for her than I was. Marissa felt she had an ally in her —someone who got up every day with the intense belief that her daughter's pain was real, who fought for her to get the answers she so very much deserved. I begrudged and resented that I couldn't fill this role. For a period of time, I placed blame for my failed marriage on the closeness and dependency my wife and daughter formed in order to survive. However, I was wrong about that. It took clinical depression, the loss of all I was clinging to so tightly, and years of hard work in therapy to realize that I wasn't that different from any of my Grace House guys. None of us are.

And now, too, I have my daughter back. All these years later, Marissa and I have rebuilt a stunningly beautiful relationship from a mound of rubble. We've experienced healing. I believe I've made amends. I watch her with awe and pride; as an adult, she's closed out accounts that no longer serve her, relearned to trust her gut. She's a courageous and wonderful woman. That's what it means to make beauty from ashes.

From Being on the Streets to Finding a Home

Before he came to Grace House, Mr. Reliable knew only anger and rage as an emotional response to being hurt, having learned it through a lifetime of burying the hurtful feelings and emotional pain that come with abandonment. Jail time only reinforced this stuffing of emotions. But at Grace House, he was learning a different way.

He had been living in an abandoned station wagon after being released from the Middleton House of Correction. He never participated in any substance use disorder or mental health treatment while incarcerated. Because he had an arson charge, committed while drunk and striking back at his attacker in retaliation for his teeth being bashed in during a barroom brawl, he was not on the classification department's priority list of those most likely to benefit from treatment. How wrong they were. When his rage got the best of him, mostly due to the harassment he received from other inmates, he would burst out in anger by verbally shouting, name calling, or hitting the wall with his fists.

At one point, this resulted in a trip to the hole, where he sat in solitary confinement for a week to ten days before being released to the streets. He had no reentry plan. He was just another statistic. In the eyes of some in authority, he was a troublemaker on the streets, who needed to learn his lesson and serve time. Though he did eventually adapt to the prison culture and became a compliant worker in the kitchen, he never was reassessed to determine if he could benefit from treatment.

I often wondered if a reassessment would have had an impact on the trajectory of Mr. Reliable's path of change. I think it might have, but the unfortunate reality in corrections is that under-resourced classification departments can only do so much. People like Mr. Reliable often get lost in the masses of inmates who just do their time, without receiving needed mental health care or treatment for the alcohol and/or drug issues that are the underlying driving forces of their anti-social behavior.

On a bitter February evening many years earlier, I answered a knock on the heavy front door of Grace House and saw Jim (who was to become Mr. Reliable) and his cellmate Ron, shivering and nearly frostbitten, standing in the shadows of the streetlight shining at the corner of Mall Street and North Common Street.

"Is this Grace House?"

"Yes, it is Grace House."

"Can we crash here tonight? We've been sleeping on the Lynnway, and it's a bitch out there. I got released from Middleton, with no money for food or a room. I haven't had a drink or done any drugs for over two years. We'll leave in the morning."

Ron left the next morning, but Jim stayed…for twelve years.

He had served a two-year sentence for an alcohol- and cocaine-driven arson charge. That's a serious charge, a shackled chain that would follow him for the rest of his life. It was not Mr. Reliable; it was the alcohol and drugs hijacking the brain and the heart of this guy, resulting in him doing things he would not do in the absence of a drug-induced brain—as is the case for hundreds of thousands who end up in our justice system because they could not manage their health condition. Mr. Reliable, and others like him, have to be held accountable for the consequences of the choices that led to their rageful behavior that crossed the line. But shouldn't we also be held accountable for turning a deaf ear to the cries for help?

His family wouldn't take him back. He was living on the streets, without food or money. He had found Grace House by word of mouth while hanging around the streets of Lynn trying to figure out his next survival move. What he found was more than a shelter for the evening; he found the home he never had. One evening of desperation led to twelve years of sustained recovery at the Grace House and another twelve years living independently from Grace House. Mr. Reliable regularly stayed in touch with me and other residents of Grace House by cell phone and occasional in-person visits.

Mr. Reliable today proudly wears the tattoo he got on his arm while a resident at Grace House. Under the two clasping hands of the Grace House logo, Mr. Reliable tattooed the words "IT'S AMAZING," signifying the bond of amazing connection and brotherhood he experienced at Grace House. He never had a home as a young adult, except jail. He got his GED in jail—one of the good things he accomplished while incarcerated. He never got his driving license, as he never had anyone to teach him how to drive. So I did. I was his coach as he wound around the curves of my Marblehead Neck neighborhood and learned how to park on our tight streets. I wondered if I'd be banned from the area if my neighbors knew I had an ex-con driving my car around the prestigious neighborhood.

Mr. Reliable's confidence grew as his driving skills improved. He often practiced with his Grace House roommate, Sonny, taking my place as coach. They would show up at my house on the Neck to just say hi. I got so much satisfaction when I saw them pull into my driveway. Mr. Reliable was proud of being able to drive; Sonny was proud to be his copilot. *Connectedness is so important for them, and for me,* I thought.

An Exception to My Rule

Sonny was one of the rare Grace House residents who never did drugs but whose problems with the law resulted from alcohol abuse and constant barroom fighting. Sonny was on federal parole and wore an ankle bracelet that monitored his every move when he was at Grace House. When his court date appeared, he asked if I would drive him to the hearing at the Moakley Courthouse, located around the corner from Boston Garden, the home of the Bruins and Celtics.

"Doc, I'm really nervous. I did a lot of drinking around the Garden during Bruins and Celtics games. I know the area, but I don't know the courthouse and don't want to ever see it again. I hope the judge lets me stay at Grace House." He explained that Grace House had become his home and he hadn't been in trouble since being with the guys at the house. "If I go back to New Hampshire, I know I'll end up drinking again. Doc, it's a lot to ask, I know, but do you think you could come in with me and say something about how I'm doing if they ask?" He explained that he froze up in court and didn't know what to say. "I'm embarrassed about how I look. Everyone will have suits on, but I don't have money to buy a jacket. A roofer doesn't need a tie or jacket."

I made it a general practice not to go to court on behalf of residents, because Grace House was not a formal program. However, I've written many letters of support over the years, with my observations about how an individual was doing in the peer-run environment. Of course, there were always exceptions to rule, based on individual circumstances. In this case, I said, "I'll drop you off and park the car in the garage opposite the courthouse. Then I'll be up and sit in the courtroom, okay?"

He smiled broadly, showing his few remaining teeth.

When we arrived at the courthouse on the appointed day, I joked with him as he opened the car door to begin his trek to the courtroom: "Grab my sport coat. If they shackle you and take you to the big house, keep the coat. I'll come for it when I visit you!"

Seeing the broad smile on his face and the bounce in his step, reflecting his confidence as he put on my sport coat and bolted up the stairs, was a reminder to me, again, how what was no big deal to me could have huge meaning to others facing the unknowns of the justice system.

As we drove home to Grace House after the hearing, Sonny was contemplative. "Doc," he said after a while, "I think they would have put me away if you weren't there. When I told the judge I was wearing your coat and you were sitting in the courtroom and were willing to speak if asked, I saw him look your way and then smile at the probation officer. I don't know what he was thinking before he looked at you, but I knew in that moment I was going home to Grace House. I'll be forever grateful to you, Doc. Thanks for being there…and thanks for the coat."

For a lot of the guys at Grace House, work was intermittent because of their record. I hired some of them to see what they could do for my properties. They started by working at Grace House, then my house, then several of my neighbors' houses after the quality of their work and their dependability had become apparent. In the process, Sonny, Mr. Reliable, Fitzy, Pat, and several others became known to my neighbors and Marblehead network of friends. As they got to know these guys as hard-working fellows, they put them to work at their houses.

Mr. Reliable got his license and bought his very first vehicle: a shiny silver Mazda pickup truck. It was his pride and joy. The Grace House Institute, the nonprofit organization I founded before starting Grace House, set up a payment plan he could afford. I hoped this would teach him how to manage his money and plan a weekly budget. Mr. Reliable had difficulty holding a steady job, even though he had stable sobriety, because he struggled with major depression that became debilitating at times. He was not able to sustain work for long. But when he worked, he worked hard and with determination, especially when he was alone painting houses.

Eventually Mr. Reliable got his own truck loan. He had certain rules for his truck: no smoking inside, no one borrows it except Dr. V., and only if it can be used for Grace House needs when Doc is driving. It was the only Grace House vehicle available for transporting guys to meetings, hauling things to the dump, etc.

When we had a party at our house on Marblehead Neck, Sonny, Pat, Mr. Reliable, and one or two trusted others with quality sobriety under their belt helped with the setup and cleanup. I noticed them engaged in conversation with some of the neighbors. I had wrongly prejudged my well-to-do Marblehead Neck neighbors. Stories emerged from some of the conversations about how a nephew, an uncle, or a cousin had a problem with alcohol and/or drugs. These super-successful businesspeople, wives, and moms were talking with Grace House guys and ex-cons, asking for their advice on how to deal with a loved one who was caught in the baffling throws of addiction. It made my heart leap with joy. If only, I thought, we could get the message out about how all these guys need people in their lives, like my neighbors, who invest in giving them a second chance.

In the Eye of My Storm

Throughout the year that followed my move into Grace House, it was a challenge to keep up the image of being a leader for my staff and continually show up for work. I was still emotionally raw, and the weight of depression was suffocating. But I was good at putting up a facade in front of others. I kept up the appearance of being in control.

I signed up for another year of racing with the crew of the *Solstice*. As we sailed by the house I once lived in on Marblehead Neck, the home I loved like no other place, I cried. My tears were agonizing and cathartic at the same time. The saltwater spray that was whipped across my face by the winds was a perfect veil and a natural soothing ointment for my tears as I stood alone on the bow getting ready to call the start line for the captain.

Time after time, this scene was reenacted as the *Solstice* positioned itself for its next race and we cruised past my home. Each time, I had to face the reality of my losses, the agony of my failure, the dreams shattered, the tormenting thoughts of "if only" and "woulda-coulda-shoulda" that served no purpose other than to punish me. But over time, my mind settled on an enduring biblical axiom that I had learned in my youth at the McCauley Water Street Mission and that had been reinforced by participating in 12-step mutual-support meetings: "This too shall pass."

It was a horrendously hot and humid day in late August. On land, it was in the nineties, but on the water, the breeze blowing at five-to-six knots was soothing. My internal reaction to the familiar scene from my old life was different this time. My stomach knotted, but it didn't do a flipflop as it had on prior sailing racing voyages. The mindfulness skills and cognitive thinking tools I had been practicing had created a negative self-talk barrier reef that insulated me from living in the past. I had gone to a lot of mutual-help peer-support meetings. I had gotten to a place of acceptance. This time as I sailed by my former home, finally, finally, I was able to think, "Tears no more." The familiar saying heard in the halls of AA and Al-Anon. "Let go and let God" had settled in. The serenity prayer had meaning to me now.

"So, Ernie," I called down to my foredeck partner, "remind me again, what is the meaning of *Solstice*?"

He said it was the two times when the sun is farthest north or south of the equator, then added, "We celebrate both."

"Kind of like being a double winner!" I said.

Ernie laughed and said, "Exactly!"

In my 12-step world, a double winner is a person who goes to both AA and Al-Anon meetings (as I had done at different times in my life) and reaps the benefits of both. Ernie and I, being foredeck crew, often had interesting conversations sitting on the rail, while the cockpit crew worked the main sheet and jib sails, and Captain Dave sailed its heading and determined the strategy for our course. The course we took and the tacks Captain Dave would call depended upon a host of variables: the direction of the wind on the sail; the keel; the tide and current; the placement of our competitors' boats; the apparent puffs of wind that would soon lift the boat, signaled only by ripples in the water; the marker we were headed for turning.

In these conversations, Ernie often related what he was last reading, and we chatted about it. Many topics were related to human behavior, societal concerns, addiction, recovery, and behavior change. Though he was a retired engineer by profession and not involved in my field at all, he made it a point to engage. Like the other crew members of the *Solstice*, Ernie was involved in life and cared about what was happening in our world and in American society. Like them, he was a compassionate conservative, though I have no idea with which political party he identified. He faced familial challenges, and in the camaraderie that occurs on the water, shared snippets of them while we sat on the rail waiting for Captain Dave's command to get ready for a tack.

A bond evolves among sailors under the challenge of competition and the demands of teamwork. I was a novice at sailing among a crew of veteran sailors, yet I had a role that was important to the success of the crew, and I was valued. I had so much to learn, and they were willing to teach me. Over time, I developed the confidence to hold my own. I could see that the seasoned crew—especially Captain Dave; John, who was an ex-collegiate hockey star; and Jack, who was a seasoned ski school instructor—took great satisfaction in my development. These guys were natural teachers who delighted in seeing the progress of a student. They also had become my peers.

The *Solstice* and its crew became like a floating Grace House for me. Everyone needs a place of refuge, and my memories of the crew remind me every day what it means to have community and how little we can do without one. So many miracles occur within a group of humans who travel a similar path. The connections found within one's peer group are an anchor for the soul. Like a solstice, I had been farthest from the light when the darkness of depression eclipsed my soul. I was brought back into the light by the healing connectedness of my peers.

10

ALEX

Caroline was a cheerleader at Roosevelt High School at the same time I was quarterback and cocaptain of its rival high school, Lincoln High School, in Yonkers, New York. Caroline was on the sidelines cheering for her team on the day of one of my biggest games. Who could ever imagine that forty years later we'd both be on the same team rooting for her son Alex?

Grace House had a rule that no pets were allowed. The community made two exceptions during the twenty years I shepherded the house in its complex, painful, and affirming journey. The first was when Piper was diagnosed with ovarian cancer and had little time to live. She had a small puppy that the community adopted so Piper would have companionship in her final weeks and days at the house. The second was when Alex asked if he could have a kitten. The house voted unanimously to make an exception for Alex. He was respected and adored that much.

I met this young, charismatic man, who had so much gentleness and so much vulnerability, through my old friend Judge Al Kramer.

"Steve, I'm calling for a personal reason."

I recognized Al Kramer's voice on the phone. We chitchatted and caught up. I was glad to hear from him but also knew something big must be going on.

"I'd like to impose upon your expertise," he said. He explained that his closest friend's son, Alex, had gotten himself in a legal jam. Due to some bad decisions he made while under the influence of drugs and alcohol, he could be facing serious jail time. Alex was resistant to treatment and didn't grasp the jeopardy he was in. His parents had tried everything for several years and hoped this latest incident could be the awakening that got their son help. He had no record. He was a Boy Scout and an average good kid in high school—what one would expect for someone growing up as the single child of two working and successful parents in Newton. "Of course, you and I know that alcoholism and drug addiction have no respect for a person's status; it's the ultimate equalizer. If you still do interventions, can you meet with my friend and his wife to discuss coordinating an intervention for their son?"

My heart broke. It always does, just a little bit, when a story makes me see again just how personal and relentless this disease can be. When you work in the field long enough, you must become a little numb but never totally numb. It's hard to strike a balance between feeling hurt and keeping one's feet moving forward.

"I'm in, Al. I'll be happy to meet with them and assess what might work for their situation."

"Thanks, Steve. This means a lot to me. I'll be in Boston next month and perhaps we can get a cup of coffee and catch up. It's a relief to know I can reach out to you."

Our conversation ended with my acknowledging his historic and pioneering contributions and expressing how honored I was to be a part of what had become a national norm for the field of drunk driving intervention. "I'm glad you reached out, Al. I'll get back to you after I meet with the parents."

Meeting Tom and Caroline

I met with Alex's parents at the Boston Park Plaza. I explained to Tom and Caroline that there is no exact roadmap for parents, family members, or loved ones of a person suffering from alcoholism or drug addiction.

"I wish I had precise answers," I said. "But each journey is an individual one. Each experience unique." I explained that my approach to interventions is a little different from what is often portrayed on television or in the media. The Accountability Training model has more of a collaborative problem-solving approach, outlining a learning and growing process of change that is ongoing, with various stages of growth and change for the entire family. I said we'd begin with an initial assessment stage in which our focus was on understanding where they were as a family, how they were affected by their son's drug use, and how they arrived at this place. I explained that we'd be working together to establish some agreed-upon goals and outcomes. I emphasized that it would be a continuous learning, growing, and action-based process involving both parents as much as their son.

The first step would involve engaging Alex so he could become more receptive to receiving professional help. However, I explained, that was only one step in the personal journey of recovery and change. There would be other goals, such as involving everyone in the family in an ongoing process of personal growth, healthy decision-making, and remaining open to change. "There is not a silver bullet in this process; it's a day-at-a-time journey of increasing one's mindfulness and acceptance of one's individual growth and change. This may sound like a lot of psychobabble, which I totally get. The priority right now is getting help for yourselves and for your son."

I also introduced Tom and Caroline to an intervention colleague of mine named Ronni. She brought the perspective of someone who was in recovery as well as the parent of an adult son who struggled with alcoholism and was in an active recovery program. "Being a double winner" is the expression often used by those who are in both AA and Al-Anon 12-step groups.

Seeing Tom and Caroline's anguish, bewilderment, and self-blame, Ronni described what we call the three C's: "I didn't *cause* it. I can't *control* it. I can't *cure* it." She explained to Tom and Caroline that even after years of working her program, this was a tool she constantly needed to recall. It would be invaluable in their work with Alex.

In *Beautiful Boy*, author and father David Sheff captures the insidiousness, infuriating, mind-boggling agony, pain, and desperation of an individual struggling to break free from the chains of bondage caused by chronic drug addiction, as well as the desperation of parents who go through the seemingly unending rollercoaster ride of trying to get their loved one help fighting this brain disease:

> "I torment myself with the same unanswerable questions:
> Did I spoil him?
> Was I too lenient?
> Did I give him too little attention?
> Too much?
> If only we never moved to the country.
> If only I never used drugs.
> If only his mother and I had stayed together.
> If only and if only and if only...
> Guilt and self-blame are typical responses of parents and other loved ones."[29]

Universal pain. No one really knows what to do with this level of despair. So we break it down into small pieces. We inch forward in the ways we can.

Alex felt he could handle his own problems. That was a familiar tune, and not unexpected, given the stage he was in. In professional jargon, we refer to it as the *pre-contemplation stage of change*. However, with those involved in the criminal justice system, I often refer to it as the *pre-pre-contemplation stage*. From my experience, the primary thinking of the offender with addiction is not "how do I change"—that's not even on their radar—but "how do I manipulate others and the system to get what I want?" Which is "get the fucking heat off me," and if in custody, "get me the hell out of this place."

I suspected that if Alex ever agreed to meet, it would be solely to get some heat off him, either from the law or from his parents. I'd seen that movie many times.

Nevertheless, with Judge Kramer involved (even though he had been retired from the bench for more than two decades), I knew it was only a matter of time before Alex would agree to meet with me. I'd seen Judge Kramer get the most resistant and reluctant person with an alcohol/drug problem to acquiesce to treatment when they did not want to do so. He may have retired from his robes, but his persuasive, articulate tough-love approach was not something that came with the clothing and the stature of the court room. Of course, the robe helped get the point across, but the person wearing the robe was the driver. Al Kramer and Andy Klein knew better than anyone I've personally known how to creatively use the leverage of the judicial system to get a person to the stage of saying yes, when all that person had on their mind was a determined "no way!"

Meeting Alex

As I drove to the residential treatment program to meet Alex for the first time, I rehearsed how I would attempt to break through his resistance. I expected a reluctant and hardcore attitude of "Okay, Doc, let's go through the motions and get this over with, so I can get my parents and the court off my back."

When I met the staff member with whom I had been in communication, she smiled and said, "Alex is wrapping up his leadership meeting and will be with you shortly.

You can have the office to the left of the stairs on the second floor."

Leadership meeting? That's interesting, I thought. No one had mentioned that to me, nor did Alex in the two preparation phone calls I had with him leading up to my visit.

I shook his outstretched hand.

"Hey, Alex, I'm Steve Valle. Most of the guys at Grace House call me Doc, but that's up to you."

"Doc works for me."

I was surprised at how friendly, engaging, and non-defensive Alex was. A tall, handsome kid with sandy blond hair and a quick sense of humor, his honesty and candor surprised me.

He put it right out there. "Doc, I don't do AA. I don't believe in the higher power stuff, and I'm not a groupie kind of person. I know I have to go to meetings to build a case so I can beat this rap, so I go. I sit in the back and daydream. Bunch of old guys telling their drunk-a-logs. I don't like Narcotics Anonymous or the young people's meetings either. I know what you're about to say, because I've heard it hundreds of times: 'Bring the body, and the mind will follow.' Not for me."

"So, you've been to hundreds of meetings already. That's impressive," I responded coyly, with a small smile.

He grinned. A little sheepish yet maintaining his confidence. "Hundreds might be a stretch, but enough to know it's not for me."

"So, do you know what would work for you? You've been in several treatment programs, seen psychiatrists and therapists. Has anything connected?" I could sense we were connecting. Alex had a way about him that pulled you into his orbit. And I was getting pulled in.

"I'm doing well here. I like the therapeutic community." He explained that he could easily pick up drugs at any time and pull one over on the staff, but he chose to say no to any offers circulating among the community. He wanted to get on with his life. Drugs get smuggled into jails and into rehab places too, despite staff's efforts to keep them out. Alex intensely asserted, "I decided to step up and take charge of the community. I told everyone I'm here because I've got to be here, but since I am here, I'm going to make my time worthwhile. If you're not into being part of the community, that's cool. But let's not bullshit each other. They voted me president, Doc."

"Cool, very cool, Alex."

We chatted for a while about his interests; his experience in Colorado, where he attended college; the program; his case coming up; and my role and the boundaries in working with him and his family. The baseline for change, in my view, is engaging the person in a genuine relationship of trust and respect. I explained that it was his choice if he wanted me to be part of his team. Entirely up to him. I told him about what I did for a living, establishing treatment programs throughout the country, and about Grace House. If he was willing, I had someone at Grace House I thought would be good to talk with—someone who'd done some serious time and knew how to work the system. I gave him Pat's number.

It had been ten years since Pat became part of Grace House. I could—and still can—recall as if it were yesterday Pat sitting in the corner of the living room with the residents at their weekly community house meeting. He had that self-assured, cocky, tough-guy demeanor I've seen hundreds of times at Grace House. His look said, "I'm here only for a little while, because I have to be, and then I'll be gone, back in the game where I know how to live."

As I was leaving, Alex shook my hand again, gave me a big smile, and thanked me for coming to see him and for helping his parents. It was clear he really loved his parents and was sickened by the pain he had caused them. "See you next time, okay, Doc," he said.

"Sure, Alex. See you next time," I said, mentally high-fiving myself. We'd made a connection. It was only a small step in the process of engagement that is essential for the change process to begin, but it was an important first step.

Staying Sober

When Alex called me about a week later and asked if I'd be willing to work with him and continue to assist Al Kramer with his case, I knew my answer. We were in: Pat, Alex's parents, Al Kramer, my colleague Ronni, and me. All of us. You can't fight this disease alone, but if you have a team, then you have a shot.

Alex was twenty-two when he left the treatment program and went to a sober house in Dorchester—Boston's largest neighborhood, steeped in tradition, customs, and diversity. Sober houses are a recent addition to the continuum of supportive housing options for patients being discharged from hospitals or rehabilitation programs, and/or released from jail or prison. Like Grace House, they are not formal treatment programs or halfway houses with some program and onsite professional staff, but do offer supportive housing in a drug-free environment.

Alex's parents went to Al-Anon and attended open AA and Narcotics Anonymous meetings so they could have a better understanding of how insidious this disease is and be educated about the hope that exists for those who choose to work on recovery. They went to counseling and various parent support groups. They read everything that could possibly help them understand how they could help their son. They made great progress in the balancing act of helping their son get reestablished, yet avoiding enabling him.

Wanting to help and not enable is the enormously difficult balancing act parents and others affected by a person's out-of-control drinking or drug use go through when they have a loved one with addiction. Tom and Caroline put everything into doing their part and worked diligently with us, taking every suggestion we offered. I admired their openness and effort to do their part and to follow the team's lead. Their pain, desperation, and hope that Alex would be able to sustain the recovery and change process kept them focused and engaged.

Alex continued with his court battle while he lived at a sober house in Dorchester and worked in the new industry of bitcoin currency. The hustle of the bitcoin industry appealed to his nonconformist and entrepreneurial side. He loved the action of it, and he was good at it, from what I could gather. I had occasional meetings with him at a Starbucks in Boston or at a local coffeeshop. On more than one occasion, he had a wad of folded-up bills in his pocket. I couldn't help but notice that they weren't small-denomination bills.

"I got this, Doc," he'd say. "I can pay for my own coffee this time and yours too."

On one beautifully clear and crisp fall day at the coffeeshop, Alex mentioned that his partner in the bitcoin business would be dropping by. "I'd like you to meet Bart, Doc. He's my meeting," he said laughing. Alex wasn't going to AA or Narcotics Anonymous meetings much and hadn't connected with anyone at the sober house either. He knew I was concerned about the absence of a support group or sponsor to hold him accountable on a daily basis. This was his way of letting me know he was fine getting his support in a manner that worked for him. "Bart doesn't use, Doc. He's okay, and he'd kick me out of the business if I was. I know that for sure."

Alex brought over my coffee and waved at the short executive-looking younger man who was scanning the coffeeshop patrons from the entrance and then hurried over to us.

"Bart, this is the Doc I told you about."

After we three had chatted for a bit, Alex reached into his jacket pocket and handed a brown bag to Bart. "Here's $2,500. We're smoking."

Alex noticed my shocked look and quickly said, while cracking up with laughter, "Relax, Doc. It's not a drug deal going down. Bart would have nothing to do with me if I picked up again. He's been through it all with me. It's all legit, Doc. Really. This bitcoin business is crazy, and the week's only half over!"

I shook my head and chuckled as they both had a good laugh at my expense. I'm an easy read, so they enjoyed the spooked look I was feebly trying to conceal.

Alex was sociable, outgoing, charming, and friendly. Yet he was also a loner. His aloneness and not going to support meetings of any kind worried all of us on his accountability team. I was, however, relieved to meet his business partner, who knew about Alex's drug-use history and would be a support while also checking on him. Alex's independent and headstrong determination to carve out his own program of recovery, in his unique way, was working for him, so we all learned to roll with it—albeit with reservations and not without worry. The angst and constant knot in one's stomach, as a result of caring for others, doesn't vanish when the person with addiction is in remission. The fear of relapse and its consequences is always lurking in the shadows of one's mind when you care for someone battling addiction.

"We gotta go, Doc," Alex said. "Lots of business out there for us."

I told Bart it was great to have met him. "I've heard a lot about you from Alex and his dad. Thanks for being a good friend to Alex. Go make your millions and have fun."

We all laughed as we said our goodbyes.

Al Kramer was successful in getting Alex's court hearing date pushed further out each time he went back to court. This was strategic on the part of Alex's legal team. The hope and expectation were that the longer Alex had to prove he was serious about his sobriety, the better he would be viewed in the eyes of the court. I think he also wanted to claim his independence from his parents and prove he could stay sober on his own, doing it his way. His strategy for staying sober on his terms and in his way was working.

Until it stopped working.

Relapse

Alex slipped after a few months of sobriety. He owned up to it and went to outpatient counseling and started seeing a psychiatrist. It was clear to us that as his sobriety time increased, his anxiety and depression, which he had dealt with in the past through self-medicating with drugs, reemerged. Most people with addiction also have co-occurring mental health issues and experience intense turmoil and severe pain trying to manage the impact of trauma. That trauma may come from their early lives or what they experienced during their drug use, living on the streets, getting involved in criminal activity, and being incarcerated. Negotiating the maze of the judicial system is fraught with anxious episodes as the person waits for the unknown to be revealed and their future to be determined by others. The process of incarceration itself is trauma inducing. For those with histories of being victimized by others in positions of power, it is a trigger for post-traumatic stress disorder (PTSD).

Alex continued to refuse to go to AA, NA, or any of the non-spiritual mutual-support meetings I had suggested. He fought forcefully for his right to do his recovery plan his way. While reluctantly agreeing to his new plan of seeing a psychiatrist and staying busy with work but not going to mutual support meetings, Al Kramer was able to get Alex to agree to a concession: if he had another slip, he would go to Grace House, under Pat's supervision.

Alex had established a good connection with Pat (who was now the president of Grace House) through occasional phone calls and meet-ups I had arranged. It was my way of preparing Alex for what I felt was likely to happen eventually. He would come to realize that Grace House was a good place for him to be, at least for a while. Call it instinct or experience, I had a gut sense he would connect with Pat, and he would thrive at Grace House. I also knew and preferred that it be his choice. I hoped he wouldn't surrender his freedom to make that choice by using again and violating his agreement with Al Kramer. Al took no prisoners when it came to the decision-making process of those in active alcoholism and/or drug addiction, and psychology went out the window if someone was actively using.

One day I got an urgent call from Tom.

"Steve, we're in Florida, but I'm a wreck!" He explained that his neighbor had called and said there was a break-in at their house in Newton. It was Alex. He had done something he'd never done before: he stole from them. He had been doing so well, living in his own apartment, making money, and having a girlfriend. Tom and Caroline thought they could relax a bit and take some time for a vacation in Florida. They trusted Alex because he was doing so well. They were coming back to Boston to assess the damage and call Al. They had no idea where Alex was but wanted to talk with me as soon as they got their bearings.

I paused and prayed while listening to Tom's pain and fear. *God, I don't want this to be happening to these people. To this good kid. With wonderful parents.*

"We'll figure it out," I told Tom. "I'm here."

Initially, you could say I was shocked. But not really. I've dealt with addiction for too long not to have already been on edge wondering and worrying about Alex. Pat and I shared our fears often when we talked about him. We had hope, but we also were worried. However, we tucked our worry away, because we knew that without some compartmentalizing, we would cease to be useful.

As soon as I hung up the phone, I called Pat and asked if he had heard anything from Alex. I briefed him on my conversation with Tom.

"I talked to him last week, Doc. He was doing great. We talked about hooking up and getting a cup of joe or a bite. Fuck it, Doc. I hate this disease and what it does to good guys. Alex is a good kid! If he makes it, he needs to come here, where I can keep him close. I won't let him out of my sight. But first we have to find him."

And we did find him.

A few days later, Alex was on the doorstep, suitcase in hand, glancing back across the common and then straight into my eyes. He held out his hand. "You knew I'd end up here, didn't you, Doc?"

I nodded as I clasped his hand.

"Welcome, buddy," Pat said. "You're finally home."

Alex was in fairly raw shape when he arrived. Normally, the practice at Grace House was for a person to complete a program after a relapse, before taking up residence. In Alex's case, Pat and the community of peers felt he had done enough treatment and that a formal rehab program wasn't the best option. It was time, Pat and the others felt, for Alex to live life on life's terms in an environment that had accountability and the support of peers, which Grace House offered. Though Alex was not in need of medical detoxification, he was hurting.

When I saw him at Grace House the next day, he was going through post-acute withdrawal—the phase of emotional turmoil, agitation, depression, guilt, and shame that is common for individuals after detoxification. Medically they are fine, but psychologically they're a mess. They are especially vulnerable for relapsing again, and the risk for overdose is high. It is a critical time during which medical and/or professional help is needed but is often denied by insurance companies because it does not meet the criterion of medical necessity. This baffling and self-defeating criterion for admission to a facility or for continuing a length of stay is simply not right, in my view. It does great harm to the individual in need of care, and it torments others trying to get help for the person they care for, whom they know could be on the verge of breaking out into a full relapse again. Families shouldn't be made to jump through multiple layers of bureaucratic red tape when they are already exasperated trying to get their loved one the care they need. Treatment on demand should be a right not a privilege available only to those with financial resources.

I was relieved and grateful Alex was at Grace House and not on the streets. After about six weeks, I could see the old Alex beginning to return. His quick wit, humor, and engaging personality were emerging once again. The other guys were connecting with Alex, and he with them. I watched a special connection emerge with Pat. He was like a little brother to Pat. He went everywhere with him, which meant he did a lot of run-around chores for the house and the guys in it. He accompanied Pat on the on-call responses Pat routinely made, getting someone a ride to detox or helping them out of a jam that could lead to a relapse. He was of service to others, which came naturally for him. He formed bonds; the guys at the house loved him.

Tom and Caroline also gave a lot of support anonymously to the residents at Grace House—dropping off groceries or giving gift cards to Pat to buy food for the residents. They were so impressed at how the residents kept the house clean and paid the daily bills, without any government grants or contracts, that they volunteered to organize a fund-raising event. Grace House had never had a fundraiser before Tom and Caroline got involved. I didn't have the skills to do it myself, and I was also reluctant to call attention to the house. However, the prodding and encouragement from Tom and Caroline helped me realize it was time to stop being so cautious and be more willing to let others hear the story of Grace House. The fund-raising event Tom and Caroline helped to organize was an enormous success, both in raising the public profile of the house and in raising money to cover the shortfall of operating funds for that year.

Robbie

The Grace House Institute had received a private donation of some computers. Alex was tech savvy, so he looked out for guys who hadn't had the opportunities he'd had growing up. He took it upon himself to set up a job resource computer lab at Grace House and to develop a computer literacy program for residents who had limited computer skills.

Robbie, who came to Grace House from the Salvation Army Rehabilitation Program's six-month work program after experiencing homelessness most of his life, was desperate for a job. Robbie could barely read; he didn't know how to type, let alone complete a job application online. He was afraid to have conversations with strangers. His frequent homelessness, stints at Sally's or other shelters, and street existence isolated him from routine socializing. His isolation contributed to his untreated depression. A vicious cycle of mood swings, being alone, and isolation created a constant cave-like existence for Robbie, with no light to find a path out. He sat at Sunday evening community meetings for weeks before he ever said a word, other than "I pass" when it came his turn to speak.

Then, out of the blue, Robbie nervously spoke up just before the circle closing. "I'm used to being on the streets, where no one cares for me. I don't know how to act here. I'm always asking myself, 'What's the angle with these people? Why do they want to help me?' No one is getting paid to help me. I know how to act and get by on the streets, but I don't know how to live like other people do.

No one showed me how. I don't even know how to live here, but I'm showing up."

Alex had great compassion for Robbie. He had a way of making Robbie talk and laugh. Though Robbie was in his fifties and Alex was twenty-three, they had a connection, a bond of caring. Alex came from a world of nurturance and opportunity. Robbie had not experienced caring people in his life, though he had been married at one time. The chasm between their vastly different backgrounds was bridged by the younger man's compassion. It was amazing to witness and so gratifying.

Alex tutored Robbie on how to complete the online application for Home Depot. He coached him on how to prepare for the job interview. He got a clean shirt and slacks from the thrift store where he worked when he was a resident at the Salvation Army Rehabilitation Program in Saugus. Pat and Alex drove Robbie to his job interview and waited for him in the parking lot. He did what the community of peers encouraged him to do: show up and try.

"Hey, Robbie," Alex shouted, as Robbie gingerly walked away from the car toward the entrance, "we got your back!"

Robbie landed a night position at Home Depot stocking shelves. His pride at having a real job for the first time in twenty years was apparent at the Sunday night community meetings at Grace House. He let others know it was because of Alex.

Alex didn't stop with Robbie. Several other Grace House residents were also able to find jobs, which they attributed to Alex. Alex brought laughter back into the parlor of Grace House. The weekly community meetings were fun again. When I stopped by the house every now and then, I saw this dynamic evolving and building. And I stayed in daily contact with Pat to get reports that validated my observations.

Alex had become our "beautiful boy."[30] Everyone gravitated to his warmth, sense of humor, youthful energy, and caring. Everyone was pulling for him. If he could fall into this disease, anyone was vulnerable. But if he could climb out, if he could fight back, anyone could.

Knowing that Grace House did not have a marketing program, Alex suggested it was important that the word about Grace House get out there. He asked if he could have the green light to see what he could do. "Doc, there is no sober house like Grace House. I've been to a lot of them. I know. You really need to tell the story about this house."

His youthful exuberance was contagious and refreshing, but I was content keeping a low profile, as had been the custom. I was in my comfort zone, accomplishing things without being noticed. (Remnants of my mom's influence, I suppose my shrink would say.) But Alex was determined, even relentless. He continued to press the idea of getting the word out about Grace House whenever I saw him or when he saw me talking to Pat.

Alex's determination and passion eventually wore me down. "Okay, Alex, go ahead. Let's see what you come up with. You know we don't have the money to invest in marketing, so I'm not sure what you can do, but go for it."

Because of Alex, the Grace House Institute received a private donation to produce a DVD telling the story of Grace House. He worked for months interviewing residents, making copy, editing, and planning the DVD.

It was while Alex was putting the finishing touches on this DVD that Michael Botticelli's visit to Grace House occurred. Alex couldn't have been more excited. He wanted to add the White House visit to the DVD. The result was a moving and compelling DVD telling the story of peers helping peers and how Grace House had been a beacon of hope for so many suffering from alcoholism and other drug addiction. We shared it with the White House drug policy staff.

Grace House, because of Alex, had moved into a new era. No longer was its light to be hidden. It was time for the Grace House story to be told and for its light to shine. In my dreams, I had envisioned Alex representing the next generation of Grace House residents and the leadership eventually being turned over to him, under Pat's firm and caring supervision. However, with the computer library room established and the DVD completed, Alex felt it was time for him to move on. He felt a sense of closure. He felt ready. I was sad and happy at the same time, but I knew it was his time to move on.

April 26, 2017

Alex stayed in touch with Pat and me. I checked in with his dad occasionally. All was going fairly well. He had some bumps managing his anxiety and depression, but with the help of medication and therapy combined, he was managing. He had an apartment, a new job, and a girlfriend once again. He was connected with his parents. He was recovery in action.

Several months went by. Both Pat and I continued to have phone calls with Alex. We made plans for a visit. That visit never happened. I was driving when I saw the familiar number appear on my cell phone.

"Doc, it's Tom."

As a clinician, as a parent, I heard the words before he uttered them: "Steve, Alex accidentally overdosed last night. We don't know the details. He was on Suboxone and doing well for quite some time. He called to let us know he was going into detox again. He sounded okay. He knew what he needed to do and intended to do it. He never made it. That was the last I heard from him, Steve."

"Tom..." But words are not meant for moments like this.

Alex was gone.

It was a monsoon of a rainstorm on April 26, that raw, early spring morning that hundreds of us mourners found parking spaces along the road at the Emet Cemetery on the Newton-West Roxbury line. One by one, we moved slowly out of our cars. The rain was pounding on us. It wasn't just raining; it was a thunderhead. It didn't matter. The horrendous weather reflected the sorrow of our hearts.

I heard a voice call out from behind me, "Steve, can you hold up a minute?"

I looked back and could barely see through my rain-pelted eyes as I turned into the wind. It was Al Kramer. The last time I had seen Al was when we gathered around the small coffee table in Grace House's computer resource room Alex had organized for the guys. It was our team meeting to discuss Alex's plans for continuing his progress whenever he was ready to leave the support he had found at Grace House. Alex was beaming with pride as he explained what he had done for the guys at the house, teaching them computer literacy and job-seeking skills.

When I hadn't seen Al at the shiva (Jewish mourning rituals) held for Alex, I wasn't sure if he had made the trip from the West Coast. I was relieved when I turned into the rain-swept wind to see his energetic bounce and curly hair jog toward me. I felt less alone.

Pat had told me he couldn't bring himself to attend, so I went by myself to the graveside service. He and I had many conversations about Alex over the days leading up to the service. I gave him a tape recorder and told him I wanted him to talk freely into it about his feelings for Alex.

Pat started talking. These are his words:

"I've been doing this for a long, long time Doc, but Alex was the only kid I ever allowed myself to get attached to.

"Alex wasn't your typical addicted person. He was a good kid. He grew up with morals, good parents. There are differences in addicted people. We had an addicted person here once, and he told the story of how every morning he would meet his mom and get in this line. All he wanted to do was drink the orange juice she was drinking. That line was the methadone clinic. What chance did he have? But that's the thing: drugs don't choose. You have two opposites, but drugs took them both.

"See, Alex was a savior. He was the kid who always wanted to help the stray dog. He was more addicted to the lifestyle than the drugs. There is a whole lifestyle involved in doing drugs. The more banged up you were and the more you were hurting, the more Alex was there for you. You see, Alex grew up with a pair of loving parents, very helpful, loving, help-anybody-in-the-world parents, and they gave him the golden heart he has. That's why I got so attached to him. It's hard to explain.

"Alex had a way about him that you couldn't resist. Any guy in the house that needed help—resumes, computers, anything—he would help. But Alex was his own worst enemy in a way. With his helpfulness and his big heart, he would help anybody, but the one he needed to help the most was the one he looked at in the mirror every day. I used to talk with him about it over and over. He had his cigarette hanging out of his lip. You could see the drugs, the lifestyle that was there, yes, but the only thing that mattered to Alex was helping. And that is what he wanted to do. I was hoping someday, maybe someday, he would become a counselor, because that is what he loved to do. He loved to help people. But the people he wanted to help were no help to him. He wasn't strong enough to help someone else; he needed to help himself first.

"I loved that kid and I miss him every day. So many drug-addicted persons are cruel, mean, all-about-me at this stage of their disease, but Alex was a gem in the rough. His lifestyle of caring was his enemy. He helped so much, but the person he needed to help the most was himself. He had loving parents and all the opportunities they gave him. It doesn't matter with drugs, though, whether you're rich or poor. Alex would see the good in anybody. He would see good when most people wouldn't. His heart was bigger than he was. And that is hard in a game like this: you get taken advantage of. Your heart gets broken a lot, especially when it comes to women in the game. If the girl was sick and suffering, that's the girl Alex wanted. Alex wanted to help everybody. And I loved him for it. To find a heart that big in this lifestyle is a very rare thing. Me myself, it has taking me years to get rid of the violence and see the good in people. Him, that's the first thing he looked for: he didn't see the bad, he saw the good.

"I guess you can say Alex was a destructive enabler. That's the blind side of the drugs. He couldn't see beyond his heart. His heart was his enemy and his best asset. I've seen the worst in addicts, and I've seen the best. And Alex was one of the best. The lifestyle of a drug-addicted person is so chaotic and so hectic that it's insanity. But Alex thrived on the insanity. He made sense of an insane world. In his mind, it all made sense. Helping other addicts was normal for him, like for me. I just do it in a different way. Alex never meant any harm; all he wanted to do was to help. He was a great kid with a great heart, who never saw the person he needed to help the most: himself. The one in the mirror.

"Alex, the one in the mirror. I love him. I think about him all the time. It's a hole in my heart that I'll never fix. To this day, I've never met anybody like him. He was truly a rare person in a lifestyle of nothing but insanity, misery, shame, heartbreak. He was light in the dark. That's why I got attached to him. Because when I wanted to cry, he made me laugh. He knew when people were hurting. He had a gift; he just chose to use the gift unwisely. Alex's heart made him want to do good things, but his mind made him do things that harmed him. That's why I truly believe this is a disease. It's a mental illness too. The lifestyle is as addictive as the drug. And when you get someone like Alex, it will drag you down. It wasn't the drugs that killed him, it was the lifestyle, and the people in the lifestyle."

Alex cared so much that his caring was his downfall.

As I walked to the gravesite, Al Kramer was walking nearby. "Bet you've been at too many of these, Steve."

"Yeah, Al. But this one is like no other for me."

"I get that, Steve."

We looked into each other's eyes, speaking no words, then turned and patted our wet hands on each other's shoulders before we walked silently toward the gravesite. The tears in our hearts outnumbered the raindrops of the rain-drenched cemetery.

Hundreds of us crouched under the tents, comforting each other from the raw rain and the broken hearts we shared. The speakers reminded us of Alex's expressions of kindness and compassion for others, such as his volunteer work at The Shrine on Arch Street and of saving a woman's life in Boston's Downtown Crossing by administering Narcan. They reminded us of his quick wit and humor. We laughed and cried and hugged.

At the end of the service, as is the custom, we grabbed a handful of soil in our hands and let it fall into the gravesite as we silently and individually bid farewell and prayed for peace.

At The Shrine's volunteer awards ceremony in 2016, Alex said, "There is something about doing work you know helps people that gives you this amazing feeling of success, even over seemingly small things. It's an experience I'll not soon forget."

Rest in peace, dear friend. You are remembered.

11

DOLLAR MAN

"Hang on, Doc." Jimmy Nine Lives jumped up off the bench we were sitting on outside South Station in Boston, sipping a cup of joe.

Before I could get a sentence in, Jimmy Nine Lives was jogging after a retreating figure in the maze of commuters who were bustling about the sidewalk in front of us. He stopped beside the forlorn-looking human, who was walking briskly, but with head pointed to the ground. Jimmy Nine Lives reached into his pocket and gave the man a bill. There was no acknowledgment from the guy. He just took the bill and charged on.

"Jimmy Nine Lives," I joked as he sat down next to me on the bench and picked up his still-steaming cup of coffee, "if I didn't know better, I'd think you just did a drug deal right in front of me."

Jimmy roared with laughter. "Never, Doc. Too much respect between us."

"So, do you know him?"

"Yes and no. I don't know his name. I see him all over the city. Today he looks pretty good. He must have gotten some clothes from Sally's thrift store. He has some sort of mental illness, like me. I know he does the right thing with the money. I've watched. He takes the dollar, never says a word, and goes and gets a burger at Micky D's. So I look for him when I'm in the city."

"Why? I mean, it's great. But you've got a lot going on yourself trying to make ends meet, right? Why him?"

"He's one person I can help. Just like we all were to you, Doc. I know what it's like to experience homelessness. What it's like to have no one care, and then to have one person care. I know what that difference feels like. I learned this from my mom. We had no money, but she found a way to care. Like you, Doc. I don't have any money, but I have a dollar. I always keep a dollar ready in case I see him. And there he was. Dollar Man I call him. He's my kindness project."

Earlier that morning, as I headed into the crowded Boston cityscape, I had wondered, *How will I recognize Jimmy Nine Lives?* Would he be in a suit and tie, stylish jeans, and sweater or would he be wearing the latest makeshift outfit off the donation rack at Sally's thrift store? With Jimmy Nine Lives, I had to be prepared for a man who could fit almost any description. He knew how to morph, how to fit in, how to survive. It is what someone learns in the space where society forgets about them.

Jimmy Nine Lives was a con's conman: a frequent flyer in America's juvenile and adult criminal justice system. His criminal career spanned three decades of periodic confinements in various reform schools, juvenile detention centers, jails, prisons, and community-based criminal justice supervision alternatives provided by dozens of probation or parole offices, all in multiple states.

Jimmy's survival skills were finely honed. All of his involvement in crimes was directly related to his drug/alcohol use and co-occurring mental health disorders. He was a nonviolent offender, as are hundreds of thousands of others like him who tragically have been incarcerated in America's prisons and jails because of their behavioral health condition and our inability as a society to see the person behind the behaviors. Sadly, in his multiple times of incarceration, Jimmy never received treatment for his addiction and mental health issues. Now, *that* is a crime.

And yet here he was, giving a dollar to a man he didn't know.

Jimmy Nine Lives survived beatings by guards, starvation, and other deprivation tactics by staff designed to force compliance or control his acting-out behavior; brutal attacks by other inmates; psychiatric medications used not to help him but to subdue him; and repeated stints of isolation in the hole. Navigating survival in the Boston Street culture was like putty in a child's palm, compared with what he had adapted to as a lifelong product of America's juvenile and adult correctional system. It was a trip to watch this man, who had endured so much darkness and yet was able to express tenderness toward a stranger.

Jimmy arrived at my doorstep about twenty-five years earlier. He had been living on the streets and was looking for a safe place to bunk down and begin again. He'd had many stops and starts—periodically being totally captive to out-of-control drinking, then being free from drugs and alcohol. He had occasional periods of sustained recovery, sometimes for many months. At times, these months strung together into a year or two or three-plus years. But a relapse was always lurking in the shadows.

Relapse is commonplace for many, but it is not inevitable. I've known many people in long-term recovery who, once they decided to stop drinking/drugging, never use again. But for Jimmy Nine Lives and many others, the risk of relapse remains high. They get stuck in a cycle of starts and stops they can't break. Or rather, I would say it is one they *can* break, but they need help. For this reason, I started Grace House. There, I got to know the many pigments that paint the mosaic of Jimmy's life journey of hell as well as healing.

In so many ways, the residents of Grace House are family, though fragmented, dispersed geographically, and often discarded by their families of origin. They identify with each other's common suffering and adversity, loss of relationships, and daily struggles as they try to survive one more day as society's castaways. Though disconnected from mainstream America, they are connected to each other's plight. This heterogeneous subculture of apparently disconnected human beings on society's fringe, due to their addiction and/or co-occurring mental health disorders and involvement in the criminal justice system, is connected by something that cannot be taken away unless one chooses to give it up. They are a brotherhood. I think about how the ripple effect of this brotherhood extends. Right now, it extends to the man and his dollar and his hamburger.

Orientation

Jimmy Nine Lives's path of suffering began when he was twelve years old. He was charged with residential burglary, not for the first time, in an Orange County, California juvenile court. All he could think about as he went before the judge was getting back home. His mother had remarried, and things weren't as bad as before. That's what Jimmy expected, but the district attorney had another suggestion. There was this new school in Utah that he wanted the judge to consider.

The judge deemed Jimmy too young and small for the California Youth Authority, and everyone in the judge's chamber agreed that something else had to be done. So a plan was proposed. The county would pay for his placement in a private "training" school for juvenile offenders if his mother agreed. But if she didn't, the judge would handle it another way. Knowing that way could be worse, his mother accepted the arrangement. Jimmy was released into her custody, with the understanding that she and his stepfather would deliver him to the reform school for juvenile boys in Provo, Utah.

Jimmy's mother had received some brochures, and everything looked great. Jimmy's expectations were high. When they arrived, he and his mom took a tour of the campus. They saw productive activities going on everywhere and a swimming pool right out front. The staff were nice, and there were pinball machines that didn't even need coins. Free pinball! There was also a gymnasium with a full indoor basketball court. Jimmy thought it was cool the judge had considered him for this opportunity. Kids came from every state, and it was very expensive: $2,500 a month. His dream was to become a surgeon, and he thought this school would give him a shot at a better education.

He was in for a big surprise.

As soon as he'd said goodbye to his family, he felt powerful arms grab him. He was led to a steel-gray door that he assumed was a closet but that led down a stairwell to what looked like a dungeon. It definitely wasn't part of the tour he had taken with his mother. He was told he was there for "orientation."

Jimmy was taken down a hallway that had a kitchen and chow hall at one end. The hallway extended about a hundred feet, then turned left, where there was a nurse's station and some other rooms. He was placed in one room. A stern-looking woman came in and told him to lie down. She explained that he'd been issued 250 hours of orientation, and that he had to earn the hours off with good behavior before he could move into the housing unit upstairs. This was called *time reduction*. Time reduction involved standing against a wall or sitting completely still with no communication, verbal or nonverbal. For one hour of standing, you got two hours of time reduction; for one hour of sitting, you got one hour of time reduction. The name of the game was to get rid of all 250 hours. Clearly it would take a long time.

Youths aged ten to eighteen were all mixed in together in the basement. The facility had no windows; everything was white cinderblocks. At night, everyone grabbed a mat and laid it end to end on the ground. There were no beds or cots. Each boy was given one flat sheet and a blanket.

In the morning, after the youths had stacked their mattresses and eaten, they were lined up against a wall. They were told to stand six inches away from the wall and shut up. Each day, they made a contract with the supervisor stating how many hours they would stand or sit. If you broke your contract, forty hours were added to your accumulated time.

On his first morning, Jimmy kept hearing his name called for an "IR." He learned that IR stood for incident report. Boys would get fifteen hours for one IR, twenty hours for another IR. Jimmy wasn't sure exactly what constituted an IR, but he could see that staff were writing up IRs as if their paycheck depended on it. All the IR tickets went into a book. That book was like the scorecard of a rained-out inning. It kept the youths stuck at the place they had entered. They were what was called "the ins." No one knew how or when they would be released to "the outs," where they could live upstairs, with more freedom of activity.

Jimmy learned quickly that IRs were given by multiple staff at a rate that couldn't be kept up with. He felt despair. Instead of teaching him, the program was set up to punish him. He had at least four hundred hours tacked onto his time before the end of his first day.

But he had yet to understand the gravity of his situation. Others were looking at him, scared, saying he'd better stop, or he'd get a "hair dance to the pee room." He had no idea what that meant. He was about to find out.

Being new and young and in the mood to test his new environment, Jimmy began to goof around. The other boys were too scared to goof around with him. It didn't take long before he had gone too far. The supervisor, who was over six feet tall and three hundred pounds, walked over to Jimmy and snatched him by his hair, lifting him off the ground. Still holding his hair, he shook Jimmy hard, then marched him down the long hall.

Another staff member was waiting. They stripped Jimmy butt naked, then opened a four-by-four plywood door with a master lock and threw him inside a small cell.

Jimmy cried himself to sleep. When he awoke, he had to pee. He cried out, but nobody would acknowledge him. He had no choice: he had to pee in the cell. The floor had dirty indoor-outdoor carpeting that had soaked up other kids' pee. Now he knew what the boys meant by a "hair dance to the pee room."

When Jimmy was let out, he was told that because he couldn't control himself, they would help him do so. They gave him an orange pill. After that, he had to learn to stand at attention. If he swayed a little bit or looked around, they said he was uncooperative and communicating nonverbally. They gave him more pills.

Jimmy was encouraged to write home. He was given a stamped envelope and paper. He wrote about everything that was going on and said he was being held underground against his will and being tortured. He begged his mother to get him out of there. Only later did he learn that his letters never left the school. Moreover, letters from his mother were shown to him but never given to him. He was told that when he had completed orientation, he could have his mail.

After nine long months, Jimmy finally got his hours down and earned his shot at the outs. He had seen other boys make it out, only to screw up and end up starting over. He determined that wasn't going to happen to him. He was going to get out of orientation, and then he was going to escape.

Jimmy knew he was near the getting out number. But he had to be careful. When their time reduction was over, the youths were given a polygraph to ask if they intended to escape or to badmouth the school. And there were other tests. One day the staff lined them up and told them some reporters were coming through and they had to be on their best behavior, or else. Jimmy was tempted to take the opportunity to scream bloody murder and get himself the hell out of the situation. But even at his age, he knew that was a bad idea. So he stayed away from the dog-and-pony show and just watched the other kids. They were too afraid to do anything but kiss ass and tell lies to the reporters. Corporal punishment and drug abuse were not mentioned that day, but claims had been made by others who had been at the school. Jimmy later learned that was one reason the reporters were there. It also later came out that the school wasn't licensed to administer drugs, yet unqualified staff were doling out drugs at will. In addition, sexual abuse was going on with younger and weaker children.

When Jimmy finally got to the outs unit, he met a guy from Alaska called Willie. They hung out and decided to escape together. The problem was that the terrain was brutal! The mountains rose up thousands of feet directly ahead of the school, and it was surrounded by woods on all sides. There were barbed-wire fences to keep animals out, but they would work both ways in any attempt to run.

Jimmy only had to get to California, but Willie was from Alaska. That was far to travel with no money, food, or water. Nevertheless, the day came, and they both decided to go for it. After their last class on a Friday, they walked the perimeter of the property, looking for a path of least resistance into the woods. The next day, Saturday, they had more free time than during the week, so they took one last look around, then ran like hell.

It was foggy and the ground was damp. They crossed a stream and their shoes became filled with water. Jimmy was leading the way when suddenly he heard Willie scream out. He turned around and found that Willie had tripped on barbed wire. Filthy and exhausted, he was crying. Maybe, he said, they could sneak back onto campus, shower up, and play it off like it never happened. But the last thing Jimmy want to do was go back. So he turned from his friend and ran.

He ran for hours, until it was near dark and he came upon a highway. He could see mountains in the far distance, but there were miles of flat land between him and them. He crossed the road and stuck out his thumb. He was afraid nobody would pick him up because he was dirty and young. Or a cop would pull up and bust him.

Finally, a trucker in a gas truck pulled over. Jimmy was excited because not only did he have a ride, but it was in a cool big rig. The driver asked where he was headed, and Jimmy said California.

The driver looked him over and said, "Where you comin' from, kid?"

Because the driver made it clear he didn't care and wasn't a rat, Jimmy told his whole story: how he'd been tortured and abused and locked in a basement for months, how he'd been called a dirty Christian and drugged and brainwashed. He held nothing back.

The road was straight and flat and boring, so Jimmy fell asleep. When he woke up, they were at a gas station in the middle of nowhere, and he was alone in the truck.

Then the driver came back and announced that this was his stop. "You'll have to find another ride, kid," he said.

Jimmy thanked him and got out. As soon as he did, the driver got back in his truck, started the engine, and pulled away—heading in the same direction. Jimmy had been duped.

Before he could get his bearings, a police car rolled up to the station. Jimmy ducked into the men's room and locked the door. He didn't want to be sent back to the school. Luckily for him, the window was big enough, so he climbed out and was off again, running. The terrain was flat as a pancake, with nowhere to hide. So he just ran.

A moment later, he saw the cruiser come around the building and head toward him. Not fast with its lights flashing—just rolling slowly, following Jimmy. The officer was wearing a big cowboy hat. He picked up his microphone and said over the speaker, "Boy, whenever you get tired, come on over here and let yourself in."

Jimmy ran until despair set in. Then he began to cry. He was exhausted and couldn't run anymore. The cop didn't say another word, never got out of his car. He let Jimmy walk for a bit. Eventually, with no other options, Jimmy got in the cruiser.

He was back in orientation.

A few days later, the director of the school came to fetch Jimmy. He hadn't seen the director since he took the tour of the school, the day he arrived. They went upstairs to the director's office. To Jimmy's amazement, his mother and stepdad were sitting there. They had been notified when he escaped and were worried sick. They'd also heard rumors about how the school was run, so they drove straight to Provo and demanded to see Jimmy.

Jimmy hugged his mom. "I have to tell you—" he started to say.

"You can tell me in the car," she said. "We're leaving!"

"Wait a minute!" the director said. "Nobody's going anywhere."

But Jimmy's stepdad grabbed the man's shirt and reasserted that they were taking their son. Then the three of them got in the car and left.

The Revolving Door

Jimmy Nine Lives told me one of the greatest days of his life was leaving that school for boys. However, being liberated from the harassment of the private juvenile facility did not release him from his court obligations. He was sentenced to finish his court sanction in a state facility under the jurisdiction of the California Youth Academy.

Jimmy was straight for a few months after he was released by the California Youth Academy. But like most offenders released to the streets, the first connections he made were with peers who are involved in drugs, alcohol, and crime. When an older kid he knew approached him and said, "Wanna do a crime with me? It will be fun," Jimmy went along with the plan. He had no intention of doing more crimes, but he was under the influence of an older, more seasoned criminal. This time, Jimmy was sentenced to five years at the California Youth Authority facility in Ontario.

"As soon as I got there," he told me, "I knew I wasn't going to make it. There were only a few white kids. I was placed in a six-man cell with five Mexican gang members. I got my ass kicked all night long. I was taken to the hospital in the morning, eyes swollen and teeth beaten back."

When he was released, at the age of twenty, Jimmy Nine Lives went right to drugs and was incarcerated again. My experience working with adult justice-involved people who have histories of involvement with the juvenile justice system as well as issues of alcohol, drug abuse, mental health, and childhood trauma has shown me that their path to normal socialization is fraught with extreme barriers. The odds of staying out of the adult correctional system are small. Jimmy Nine Lives couldn't beat the odds.

A few years later, Jimmy had another encounter with the criminal justice system, this time as an adult in the Old County Jail (OCJ) in Santa Ana, California. A series of rough experiences taught him about the codes that exist behind the walls. It is another world, another society, with subcultures existing within subcultures. Lines of division based on race, age, sexual orientation, and whatever crimes you are in for exist within each corrections facility. This has changed to some degree over the years as a result of reforms of professional standards and accreditation processes, but the criminal justice system is still a dangerous place to be, no matter how well facilities are run, who you are, or how you play your cards.

By the time Jimmy Nine Lives was in his thirties, he had been in about a dozen prisons in five states, adding up to twenty years in institutions, jails, and prisons—nearly all of his time related to untreated addiction and co-occurring mental health disorders. Jimmy never had an opportunity for substance use disorder treatment or the co-occurring mental health disorders he had struggled with since his youth. Never. This sounds like it should be the anomaly. That would be common sense, right? The hard facts are that less than 15 percent of the prison and jail population receives any form of substantive treatment for addiction and mental health issues, even though over 80 percent of inmates have serious problems with alcohol, drugs, and/or co-occurring mental health disorders.[31] And we wonder at the revolving door.

"I had no preparation for going out either," he once told me. "I was once offered a halfway house, but I told them, 'Are you kidding me? Why would I stay in a halfway house after being locked up for so long?'" This resonated with me and caused me to think hard about the knee-jerk reaction we professionals have of placing released inmates in another institutional setting. They do need a safe place to go—one with some structure and definitely where they are held accountable—but do they need another institution-like setting?

"I became institutionalized, Doc," he said. "I had no fear of prison or jail. I was used to it. It didn't matter where the jail or prison was, I could fit in anywhere. I couldn't break the pattern, so why not just make it work"?

Miracles Happen

Yet miracles do happen. I have come to believe in miracles because of the evidence in the lives I've witnessed while working with people who recover from active addiction and mental health problems in all kinds of healthcare and public safety settings. Also, my experiences at Grace House and every time I show up at a 12-step meeting have shown me that miracles happen all around us.

When I was about the same age Jimmy Nine Lives was when he escaped from the horrors of juvenile detention in Utah, I led services on many Saturday evenings at the McAuley Water Street Mission as part of an outreach effort by my church youth group. I was touched by the river of sadness emanating from the men in the stark makeshift pews before me. I couldn't wait till the service was over and I could mingle with the men while they waited for their daily bowl of soup. Other kids in my youth group hung with each other, and the leaders mingled with the mission staff. Not me. I was young, naïve, and totally unaware of the depth of human brokenness and suffering experienced by the unshaven, smelly, poorly clothed men who had come inside from the bitter cold to get their home-cooked meal for the day.

For many who were experiencing homelessness, this was as close they would get to home ever again.

I wanted to ask what their day was like; how long had they been coming to the McCauley Water Street Mission; whether they had any family; and if they did, when they last saw them. What kind of jobs did they have, and what ones did they like? I was curious, but more than that, I wanted to see if they had a spark of hope left inside their rugged exterior.

I'm sure I was regarded as naïve and maybe offensive by some. After all, I was only fourteen or fifteen. But most of the men seemed to genuinely appreciate my feeble and awkward efforts to relate to them. I could tell by the wave of a hand or slight nod of a head when the men filed into their rows, anticipating the hymn singing and gospel message, and of course the meal that awaited them.

These men at the mission had no money to buy dinner, but they did have to pay a price before they could receive their nourishment: they had to sit through a gospel service. If they didn't, then no hot meal for them. Something about this didn't sit right with me. I felt it cheapened the gospel message by making conditional what Jesus taught was unconditional: God's love and grace for all of humanity. Believe first, eat later? It didn't seem right to me, but what did I know? I was young, and my role was to be of service by preaching the gospel of forgiveness, change, and redemption, and by helping to serve a meal. Nevertheless, the seeds of questioning and challenging prevailing norms and beliefs were being sewn in the tarnished soil of humanity I met at the McAuley Water Street Mission. I got more from my personal exchanges with these men than I ever gave from the pulpit. What I learned made a lasting impression that shaped my career path and my own life's vision and mission. It lit a fire within that could not be extinguished by time or experience; it still burns within.

Was it a coincidence, I wonder now, that my first job after obtaining my master's degree in rehabilitation counseling was as a counselor in the Salvation Army Rehabilitation Program in Providence, Rhode Island? Was it a coincidence that Jimmy Nine Lives found his way to Grace House after being a resident of Sally's in Saugus? Was it by chance that I made the choice to turn my home into a home for ex-cons with an addiction and co-occurring mental health disorders who had no home? Did my early experiences have anything to do with why I felt connected to Jimmy Nine Lives and many of the other residents of Grace House or those in jailhouse jumpsuits I saw in the jail and prison programs I directed? Were these coincidences? Or "God-incidences," as they say in AA? Or karma?

For me, it's all part of spirituality. I see spirituality as a foundational principle upon which meaningful recovery is built and sustained. Jimmy Nine Lives found it in his own way with Dollar Man. I was linked to Jimmy Nine Lives, and Jimmy Nine Lives was linked to Dollar Man. I sometimes wonder how far those ripples travel.

12

"Don't Stop Believin'"[32]

Transformation of any kind tends to come with discomfort and more than a bit of grief, but finally brings us to a deeper and more loving, hopeful, honest humanity.[33]

Though it's been over twenty years since I first met many of the individuals I have written about, many still stay in touch with me. When I hear from them—whether by phone, text, email or in person—it lights up my day. When I was going through my shadow period, battling clinical depression, the connections with these Grace House family members sustained me.

So where are they now? Here are some snippets of conversations I had with those who remained spontaneously connected to me over the years. Yes, out of the synergistic interweaving of the new law of three forces (accountability, community, respect), new arisings continue. It can be turbulent at times, and imperfect for sure, but the forces of transformation continue to be present in these lives.

Omar

"You are covered by prayer" greeted me via text message as I awoke from a night of on-again-off-again sleep. The 12:39 a.m. text was another reminder from Omar, one of many uplifting and kind reminders that randomly but consistently appeared over the twenty-plus years since Omar left Grace House, and the ten years since I last saw him in Las Cruces, NM. Most of the messages were left as voicemails, as I was often in a facility when he called. As technology advanced, the messages were also by text. They were reminders that I am not alone.

I responded to Omar's text an hour or so later: "As you are also, Omar. God bless."

Another time, I was having my morning coffee and preparing to join an online Palm Sunday church service as the ping alert sounded, notifying me that a text was waiting. It was from Omar. It was a Palm Sunday like no other. Because of my recent travel, just as the COVID-19 outbreak was entrapping our nation, and because I was experiencing some cold symptoms, I was self-isolating in Brewster, on Cape Cod. I had returned from a speaking engagement at a major conference in Washington, DC, on the opioid and other drug overdose epidemic. The overdose epidemic is only getting worse as the world grapples with the horrific pain, loss, and suffering of the COVID-19 pandemic. The tentacles of addiction know no boundaries.

Looking down at the text, while I sipped my morning cup of coffee, I read, "Good morning, sir. God bless you.

I'm trying to be the light you were talking about. Stay encouraged. God bless you, sir."

And a light he is. Omar had crisscrossed the country looking for work and a place to settle down after the incident I described that took place many years ago on Adams Street in Lynn. He lived in North Carolina for a while, then Texas. He was divorced from his first wife, whom he had married in the quaint Marblehead Grace Community Church we attended together during his Grace House days. We kept in frequent phone contact throughout the years. The positive, caring, and uplifting messages of encouragement left on my voicemail made my heart leap with joy and put a smile on my face.

During my darkest hours of struggling with my own losses, emotional pain, and depression, Omar's messages often lifted me out of despair:

"Doc, it's the big guy here…remember…He makes a way out of no way."

"Big guy here, checking in…be blessed, Doc. Keep Him first. Be blessed. Talk to you later."

He sent dozens of messages over time. Somehow, they always came at a time when I needed them most. His messages never failed to have a reassuring and calming effect on me, in a manner that my psychotropic medications, as helpful and necessary as they were, could not. The human connection—the bond created by shared pain, faith, and hope of a better tomorrow—traversed the neurochemistry of my brain and reached my soul.

Omar had such an impact on my life that I took a side trip from a professional conference and finally agreed to his frequent requests that I visit him at his Las Cruces home. I met his coworkers at Walmart, where he worked; his wife; his parents; and an aunt whom I had met at Grace House when Omar was a resident. The family rolled out the carpet for me. Omar insisted that I cancel my hotel reservation and stay with them. After church services with his small Assembly of God congregation, his mom put together a big Sunday dinner and invited about twenty others to the house to "meet the Doc." I felt humbled and touched by the whole experience. Joy and warmth permeated the living room as we all sat around the fireplace eating and sharing.

About nine years after that epic visit to Las Cruces, my cell phone rang as I was leaving a supervision session with my staff at a correctional treatment program in Massachusetts. When I saw Omar's name light up my screen, I knew my day was about to be made brighter. Omar's monthly calls, voicemails, and text messages always had that effect on me.

"Doc, you ready for this?"

"Hey, big guy, it's good to hear your voice. How are you and Nicole doing?"

"God is good, Doc. It's hard, you know, losing my mom. And my stepdad is in a senior care home now. But we're handling it. Nicole has her degree now and she's doing home visits and such. But get this..."

"I'm all ears."

"I'm a deacon! They made me a deacon of my church! The one you went to with me years back. Can you believe that, Doc? Me a deacon!" Omar laughed so loud I had to pull the phone away from my ear.

"Deacon Omar. That just sounds so right. Congratulations. Your light continues shining bright, big guy. Amazing Grace, eh?"

"You're so right, sir."

"God bless, big guy. Hugs to Nicole. Please tell her I absolutely love listening to the T.D. Jakes CD she gave me when I was pulling out of your driveway!"

Yes, I thought, just as I had thought when leaving his house in Las Cruces nine years earlier. I was reminded once again that miracles do indeed happen. Omar, in living out the words of the Old Testament prophet Isaiah, traded "ashes for beauty."[34] His life epitomizes the new arising that comes from living out the new law of three. He is truly a miracle of recovery and a model of transformational change.

Elvira and Jimmy Nine Lives

Elvira has had many years of success as a sales representative in the drug-testing industry. She and Jimmy Nine Lives, her partner since leaving Grace House, have lived together off and on in several East Coast communities, depending on her work opportunities. Elvira practices her recovery program by being of service to others. She has been on the board of directors of the Grace House Institute for over a decade and stays close to her recovery support community wherever they live. Jimmy could always find work wherever Elvira's profession took her.

When they were together and Jimmy was sober, they enjoyed each other and lived a meaningful lifestyle of helping others in recovery and loving and being of support to each other. When Jimmy lapsed into drinking, which occurred periodically, Elvira held to a tough love standard: "Stay sober or get help and complete a treatment program if you want to continue in this relationship."

I had text and phone conversations with Elvira and Jimmy over the years and was a witness to their deep, loving, yet yo-yo relationship. They had many years of recovery and service, and many times when life was hard and they were struggling. Through thick and thin, they remained committed to each other and always seemed to "find a way out of no way." They believed in each other and in not giving up on their relationship, though it was sometimes on very thin ice. They never gave up.

After some years of sobriety, Jimmy relapsed and started drinking again. He couldn't stop drinking, and his health was deteriorating badly. He couldn't walk without assistance and was frail. At one point, he mentioned that he had cancer. They were in fear of losing their home and all they had worked for. Elvira and I worked together to intervene in his cycle of uncontrollable drinking and attempted to get him into a treatment program. He eventually did comply with Elvira's demands to get help.

Elvira sent me this text message:

> Hi Dr. Valle. I have an update but it's not that great. Jimmy had a conference call yesterday with his sister and the psychiatrist at the facility. He's talking out of both sides of his mouth—he said that he still wants to drink but he's also saying that he has a plan for suicide and that he means to do it. The doctor of

course is suggesting that he at least stay there for 30 days. I am almost positive at this point, since he's making statements about suicide, that they would automatically have to keep him. The good news is I have his debit card, so he's really not gonna get far. I will keep you posted. Have a great day. I'm still praying for a miracle…just the fact that we got him out of the apartment is huge. God had a big job there!!! Lol.

My response to Elvira:

I'm praying for another miracle too! His life is full of them. From his youth and his entire adult life, I've never seen such resiliency and survivability as he displays. I'm hoping he has some more "one day at a time" recoveries in him. If they keep him for a month or so, that will be huge for him to build a foundation to start over, once again. He knows the drill, Elvira. If anyone can pick themselves up off the mat after being knocked down, Jimmy can. If he does stay in the program, I'll be able to talk to him once he is sober. Stay strong. You're an amazing woman, Elvira! So much respect for you! Hang tough.

Elvira thanked me for my response, saying it was hard to find people who commit to something and stay committed, and who understand the challenges of staying in recovery. Over the next few months, she kept me updated on Jimmy's progress. He had made it to a sober house. She joked that his name was now going to be Jimmy Ten Lives.

After Jimmy had spent a few months at the sober house, I heard from Elvira again. She said it had been a tough year, but he was doing better. They'd moved into a safe place that would offer security for the years to come. It had an elevator and other amenities. "I guess," she quipped, "this officially makes us senior citizens! We always wanted to move into a place like this—just didn't know it was gonna happen so quickly."

So, some twenty years after we met, Elvira and Jimmy started another chapter in their lives. They'd been on the mountain top and muddled their way through the low valleys. When they got knocked down, they kept getting back up to face another day. What was so amazing to me was how, even in the darkest of times, they managed to keep a grateful attitude, a sense of humor, and a steadfast faith that things would turn out okay. They were a model of imperfect resiliency, hope, and perseverance.

On Thanksgiving 2021, Jimmy Nine Lives left me this voicemail:

> Hi, Dr. Valle. Thank you so much for helping us. We are cooking a turkey in our new apartment. Actually, we got it for free at the last minute. We don't have much cooking supplies, because we're still fighting to get our stuff back from the landlord, but we're grateful for what we do have and so grateful to you for you helping us. Thank you and have a wonderful holiday with your family. We love you. Pictures of our apartment to follow. We got one of the biggest units here. It is two efficiencies made into one, and it has a total of six closets, which we are

loving. We have gotten some help with furniture, which is temporary, from Friends of the Poor, and we've gotten some great stuff online from free sites including the turkey I went and got last night at 11 p.m. after I got done working! Thawed and ready to go. We are feeling pretty good and we're grateful. Just wanted to touch base again. Thank you so much. Sorry it took us awhile to get in touch, but we have been trying to take care of everything all at once. I ain't even got the words, brother… praying without ceasing. What else do we have besides each other and God? Thanks, V-dog. Really good to know someone cares…like I said…Thanks. Love you, Dr. V.

We kept in contact periodically over the next several months as they continued their battle to retrieve possessions the landlord had confiscated in lieu of back rent. Elvira and Jimmy Nine Lives were outraged at the landlord for lying and spreading false rumors about them being delinquent in their rent. They took great pride in paying their bills and were greatly offended by the landlord smearing their reputation. They took the landlord to court, as they felt they had not been treated fairly or with respect. I wrote a letter to the court attesting to their character and strong sense of responsibility. They told me they planned to move into a new apartment once they had received their belongings from the previous landlord. Things were looking up for them.

But then, in May 2022, I heard from Elvira. She had horrible news. Jimmy had passed away unexpectedly. He went to sleep in his recliner, and she found him there deceased the next morning. The multiple health problems he had struggled with had taken its toll.

I was stunned and saddened. I knew Jimmy had been suffering for a long time with multiple serious illnesses, but I somehow expected that he'd have another nine lives. He always did. Our conversation fluctuated between tears and laughter as we shared memories of the man we both loved. I told Elvira I had no doubts Jimmy was totally embraced by the love that is beyond our comprehension. He knew of that love and lived it out—imperfectly, of course—in this life, and now he is in the perfect peace that passes all understanding.

Over the decades I knew Elvira and Jimmy Nine Lives, their spiritual compass always pointed true north in practicing respect, kindness, and service to others, no matter what dire circumstances they found themselves in. They lived out the principles of accountability with each other and the community with whom they were connected, wherever that might be. They knew how to "keep coming back."

Sonny

"Addiction is a complex brain disease."[35] A common realization in the addiction treatment field is that relapse is often, though not always, a natural part of the recovery process. Unlike for Pat, Omar, and Elvira, who have maintained long-term sobriety (more than ten years), for Sonny, relapse was frequent. His six years at Grace House were his longest period of uninterrupted sobriety.

Every few months, I would get a call from Sonny. For about two years, the calls reflected a grateful and sober person, but that changed when he started drinking. I heard less often from him.

In April 2020, I got a call: "Hey, Dr. V., is this you?"

"Yes, it's me. Is this Sonny? I'd know your voice anywhere, even though it's been about a year, maybe longer, since we last talked. Where the hell have you been hiding out these days? In some cabin in the New Hampshire woods?"

"I'm still up here in the boonies, where I like it. You know me. Even at Grace House meetings, I never spoke up much. I'm a loner, always was. Well, except for the women, of course," Sonny said, laughing out loud.

I laughed with him. And then there was silence.

"Dr. V., you know, I tested positive for the virus. I went to the hospital and got a test. But I'm good now. I got the antibodies in me. You wouldn't recognize me. I'm two hundred pounds. I'd never fit into your sport coat now! I'll never forget you coming to the federal courthouse in Boston with me. My only trouble was when I'd be drinking and get into fights at the bar. That's why I did time; those bar fights were nasty. But at Grace House, no way would I use, so I was cool. The truth will set you free."

"And the truth did set you free, didn't it, Sonny? You proved them all wrong. What did you end up having for sober time at Grace House, about six years, wasn't it?"

"Yup, six years without a drink or any pills. I've got my girl coming over soon, and we're going to chill a bit. I've got gratitude. A grateful heart never bleeds, Doc."

"You sound pretty chill, Sonny. I remember when you used to end Grace House meetings by saying, 'A grateful heart won't use.'"

"Yeah, Doc. Can't lie to you. Got too much respect for you. I got a can of beer right now. You know that, I'm sure. But I never did drugs, never put a needle in my arm. I'd never lie to you."

"You've always been straight with me, Sonny. Even when it hurts, you tell the truth. I know that about you. You're an honest guy."

"You got that right."

"I know you are a tough live-free-or-die type of New Hampshire independent and honest guy. I get that. But when you're drinking, all your good intentions go down the drain with one bad decision. Right, Sonny? I'm glad you're not in bars where you'd end up in a brawl sooner or later and that you're being smart by not driving."

"I'm staying out of bars, and my girl does the driving. I left that life of trouble behind. I'm getting back to work soon, when the weather breaks and I can get on a construction crew."

"That's good. You're real talented with a hammer in your hand. Have you been in touch with anyone from the house lately? Pat or Jimmy?"

"Do you have their numbers? I lost them. I'll give 'em a call."

"You know, if you want to get back on track, Pat, Jimmy, or I will be there in a heartbeat. We'll get you to a detox. You put six good years together at Grace House. You can take that first step again. Here are their numbers. Reach out to them. I'm glad you haven't lost my number."

"Hey, if I need you to stand up for me again, can I call you?"

"What do you think, Sonny?"

"Yeah, I know you would," Sonny said, laughing as his voice faded. "I love you, Dr. V."

Mr. Reliable

I was in Boston's North Shore area this past holiday season and gave one of my usual check-in calls to Mr. Reliable. I typically got a short check-in text from him every few weeks.

In a recent chat, I asked if he was still reading the Recovery Bible I gave him years ago, which he read diligently at that time. In his better times, it was the primary occupant of the passenger seat in his impeccably kept truck. He mentioned that he had lost his Recovery Bible when he lost his truck, so I ordered a new one for him.

Mr. Reliable had been living alone in a community development housing project since his wife passed. He only had his social security check and food stamps to live on, but somehow, he got by. His dog was his primary companion until she passed a couple of years after his wife.

I knew well Mr. Reliable's propensity for periods of severe depression, so I tried to keep in constant contact with him, as did Pat. He was in a very vulnerable time, following the loss of both his wife and pet. Mr. Reliable could get in some very scary dark spaces when depression consumed him. Pat and Mr. Reliable didn't have the comradery of Grace House any longer, because they lived in different cities, but they had their cell phones—a critical component of survivability for many released prisoners or probationers.[36]

I was always concerned that neither Mr. Reliable nor Pat went to AA meetings with any consistency, but they are examples of people who maintain sobriety by means of different pathways. Mr. Reliable went about twenty-one years before he had a three-day slip after his wife's funeral. For Pat it had been over fifteen years since he left prison and found himself at Grace House.

Pat confided in me on several occasions that he expected to just need a few weeks of transition at Grace House. Once he had accumulated enough money from his job as a helper on a Sally's truck after his release from prison, he would "get back in the game." Those few weeks turned into over twelve years and a life of giving unselfishly to others at Grace House. Pat always held Mr. Reliable accountable and was there for him when Mr. Reliable was in crisis, whether at the house or in the years thereafter. The three of us developed our own little community of peer support over the years. It sustained us and kept us connected.

Walker

Walker took the courage and commitment to recovery he displayed that pivotal day on the TRAC unit at Middleton House of Correction, when he stood up to the negative element on the cell block, and applied it to business and in service to others. He started his own technology business and has made it a success. He volunteers his time and expertise as president of the Grace House Institute.

I reach out to Walker for advice and consultation when other former residents contact me. When former residents were on the threshold of experiencing being without a roof over their head or lost their jobs due to the COVID-19 pandemic lockdown, Walker stepped in to help. He sent me this email when I became aware of the urgent need to support former residents and brought it before the Grace House Institute's board of directors:

> Hi Doc, I most certainly remember it being an impossibility to come up with first and last month's rent. I barely had $5 left over after every week of work. I worked at minimum wage for 3+ years (at Boston Sports Club!) while going back to school. It took me another couple of years of savings to get my own apartment. I still frequently have bad dreams of being held against my will. (The situations change, but the theme is always the same: jails, institutions, or something similar. There is most definitely a PTSD component to being incarcerated.) My thoughts are with Elvira and Jimmy Nine Lives. I hope this helps get them out of the tough spot. Sometimes it is the littlest things that can adjust the trajectory of a bad situation and turn it into a life-changing event.

Emails like this and another brief text like the one below are reflective of dozens of conversations I've had with Walker over the years:

> Today I had jury duty. I can't believe I got picked to serve on a jury in a criminal trial. Had the full interview with the judge, DA, and defense attorney. Sat the whole trial, was a main juror, led the discussion during deliberation and delivered the verdict. What a mind bender to think that the judge, the DA, and defense all agreed that I should be paneled.

Over the years, I have talked with Walker many times about sharing the stories in this book, as well as his story. It was Walker who came up with the phrase "From Chains to Change." I made note of it at the time, and years later I found the note—just as I was wrestling with what to use for the title. I decided to go with Walker's impromptu suggestion, reflecting my inclination to trust the instincts of those who have "been there, done that." For me, it was another God-incidence.

Ryan

Since returning from California and spending a night on the couch of Grace House to attend a court hearing for custody of his daughter, Ryan has lived in the Boston area, working as a professional chauffeur and raising his daughter. He loves being a dad and exudes positivity in everything he does. When I occasionally hear from him in a text message, he typically follows that with a brief conversation. He always lifts my spirits and makes me laugh. I'm sure his charming Louisiana twang and polite mannerisms are a valued asset in his profession as he drives people around Boston. He is an awesome dad to his daughter.

Danny

Danny has built a successful career as a real estate professional in Boston's North's Shore area. He has been a present and proud dad to his daughter and is a respected professional in the business community. His long-term sobriety (over twenty years) and the way he lives the new law of three in his personal and professional lives is a testament that transformational and enduring change is possible.

I haven't had as much contact with Danny as I have had with some of the other former residents of Grace House, but I always get a Christmas card with a photo of him and his daughter, often with a short note. I look forward to his card as if it were from my own family. When Danny was a resident at Grace House, his daughter was quite young. Through the yearly Christmas photos, I've watched her grow into a teenager. The pride and joy in Danny's expression is evident.

I was strolling the downtown streets of Salem, Massachusetts, on a crisp fall day, a bustling high energy emanating from the tourist crowd visiting this historic area, when I bumped into Danny. He was on his way to a real estate showing and looked dapper and professional, with a confident bounce in his step. I wasn't surprised at that. While a resident at Grace House, he always dressed well and took pride in his appearance. He also stood out among the residents as the professional businessman, so his peers selecting him to serve as treasurer was a no-brainer. When Danny was in charge of the finances, I had full confidence everything would be in order.

He spotted me out of the crowd and called out my name. "Dr. Valle, over here!"

We had a great, short conversation in which he updated me on his career and his daughter's development. His pride in her cast a beam of joy as he spoke.

I feel I can bump into Danny at any time or place, and it will be as if time stood still. Such are the bonds formed through the connections at Grace House.

Tom and Caroline

In my forty-year career in addictions, mental health, corrections, and private clinical practice fields, I have met many parents who lost a son or daughter to a substance use disorder, mental health disorder, and trauma. Some had sons or daughters who died from an accidental overdose, like Alex; for others, it was suicide or illness. However, many were able to establish a lifestyle of recovery and dramatically transform their lives. I have laughed and cried with these parents and shared their agonizing trauma, never-ending emotional rollercoaster of hope and despair, and unpredictable swings of intense anger and glimpses of exhilarating joy—all accompanied by a paralyzing helplessness and the ever-present haunting chorus of "what if" and "if only" that rents space uninvited in their minds. These parents' lives are a continual solstice of endings and new beginnings.

As Alex became embedded in Pat's and my heart during his residence at Grace House and afterwards, so did his parents. Tom and Caroline were a constant support behind the scenes of Grace House—contributing time, talent, professional contacts, and resources to help the house and the residents, always anonymously. After Alex's passing, that did not end. A computer room and library, which we called "Alex's room," was made possible because of Tom and Caroline. Pat personally renovated the room we named in honor of Alex. It was his grieving and catharsis project, I believe.

In 2017, I received several texts messages from Tom after I updated him on the progress of Pat's library renovation project:

> This is wonderful to read. Alex loved Pat. It is so comforting to think they are still connected. Grace House is remarkable. Alex had every loving opportunity to thrive there and, briefly, he did. My regard for the place, however, is not dependent upon my gratitude for what it did for Alex. I just admire it for what it is: independent. Fearless. I'm glad that Pat is taking on this project. I know Pat will capture the essence of Alex's presence in the makeover. Grace House is a place of miracles for many.

After some time, Caroline felt a calling to be part of something that would help other parents. She became an integral member of Team Sharing Inc., a national organization of parents who have lost a child to addiction. According to its website, Team Sharing, a national organization of parents who have lost a child to substance abuse disorder, is a resource that provides "support and friendship to grieving families, while working to raise awareness of substance use disorder and its impact on our communities."[37]

When my godson took his own life recently, after years of battling addiction, mental health disorders, and the trauma of incarceration, I was in turmoil over the loss and how I could be of help to the grieving parents who are also my dear friends. I turned to Caroline for guidance. Because of the community and bond of connectedness as formed at Grace House between Tom, Caroline, Pat, and me, I was able to offer Team Sharing as a resource to my godson's parents.

The grief and loss due to Alex's accidental overdose doesn't take away the broken heart and empty space that will always exist, but helping others, as Carolyn and Tom model so poignantly, does help in the healing process.

Many Others

Over the twenty years I served as shepherd for the peer-change model for recovery, scores of lives crossed the threshold of Grace House. The stories of Omar, Elvira, Mr. Reliable, Ryan, Danny, and Pat are but a sampling of the transformational changes that occurred. There were also, for example, Fitzy, Letitia, Sonny, Jimmy Nine Lives, and Terrell, whose lives were a rollercoaster ride of intermittent episodes of sobriety and slippage into relapses, with sometimes dire results. However, they somehow managed to pick up the pieces and recover from the wounds and hurts of their relapses and have periods of good stability and cohesion. Sometimes it lasted for months, other times for a few years.

Tragically, there were others for whom their last relapse was final. After Alex, Mikey, Scottie, Frankie, Paul, Robbie, and others left the peer support of Grace House and stopped following their program of recovery, a relapse into drug use resulted in an accidental overdose or suicide. We honor them for the time they shared their struggles and their lives with us and for the courage they displayed in battling this vicious disease of addiction and co-occurring mental health disorders and trauma-impacted lives. We appreciate them also for those they tried to help along the way, even when they were not able to help themselves.

As for me...

Keeping in mind that "to everything there is a season, and a time to every purpose under the heaven,"[38] one of the most difficult decisions I've had to make at this stage of my life was to accept that my time for owning and operating Grace House had come to an end. It was time for another solstice in my life. The hundreds of people who crossed the threshold of Grace House helped shape me into the person I am. Of all the special moments I've had running programs in prisons, jails, healthcare, and justice system settings for four decades, the relationships with the Grace House residents are the most memorable and impactful. Many of these men and women are a core part of my life, and I am grateful and blessed to know them.

I did not want to step away, yet I was nearing the age of retirement, with all the unknowns that implies. I realized the time to pass the baton had come. I had hoped to find a buyer who would carry on the mission of Grace House and maintain Pat as the live-in house president. It was a bittersweet moment for me. Though Pat made extraordinary attempts to work with the new owner to keep Grace House going, it did not work out.

"Doc," he told me, "it's just not Grace House anymore. The guy just doesn't get us."

I told him it was okay. Grace House is not about a building; it's about the heart. His heart, my heart, and the tapping into the hearts and the power that exist in the peer-support community. I said, "You have a passion for helping others, especially young men like Alex, and if there is a new season for Grace House in another location, we'll be led to it. The calling will be self-evident. Our job is to stay open, honest, and willing. Right, Pat? Let's be looking for the next venue to carry the message forward and let's keep the memory of Alex close. We know Tom and Caroline are on the team supporting your vision, as I am, along with other former Grace House residents and supporters."

"Yeah, Doc," Pat said, "it is about the heart. If it's meant to happen, it will."

It is in the process of being accountable to help others by sharing our experiences and stories that communities of connectedness are built, and spirituality is nurtured. Living this new law of three as best I can by sharing my story of recovery from clinical depression, the life lessons I learned from the residents of Grace House, and the spiritual gifts I receive from practicing my program of recovery and service is now my third calling. In so doing, I want to offer hope that recovery from mental health disorders, substance misuse, and trauma is indeed possible, and that transformational change is attainable. In living and working among these imperfect, wounded, flawed lives over the course of my career, and in telling my story, may a glimpse of the divine hidden within us humans be revealed.

In the words of Jimmy Nine Lives, "So I believe what it all comes down to is being kind to one another. When kindness is shared with zero motive, that is the ultimate love."

Acknowledgments

My life has been blessed with the presence of key mentors and models who influenced my personal, professional, and spiritual growth and who were there for me at pivotal times in my development. Particularly, Jack Sidebotham, Manny Lopes, Iowa Senator and Governor Harold E. Hughes, Massachusetts State Representative Kevin Fitzgerald, and Charlie Powell. Though no longer with us, they remain with me, and the many precious memories we shared continue to remind me of how to live a life that matters. Their true-grit, courageous, authentic, all-embracing, nonjudgmental, and non-dogmatic spirituality modeled for me what genuine faith is all about. I honor them, cherish the times of joy and sadness we shared, and miss them dearly.

I've always taught my staff that effective and meaningful change programs can only happen when the organizations in which we provide recovery and change services have champion leaders at the helm of the organization. Five leaders were especially outstanding, and the programs we established with them were groundbreaking and became standard bearers for excellence: Sheriff Frank G. Cousins, Jr., Essex County, MA (retired); Sheriff James M. Cummings, Barnstable County Sheriff's Office, Bourne, MA; Mike McCarthy, former chief financial officer (CFO) Essex County Sheriff's Department and current CFO for Northern Essex Community College, MA; Massachusetts Acting Commissioner of Probation Dr. Ronald P. Corbett (retired); and Ric Ohrstrom, founder and chairman of C4 Recovery Solutions, Inc. These colleagues are recognized thought leaders and chief executives in their respective disciplines who have made outstanding contributions in leading, educating, and changing organizations to be more responsive in helping people find recovery from substance use, trauma, and mental health disorders. They have been instrumental in my professional development and career, and I am grateful for their fearless, caring, and creative leadership. I also wish to acknowledge Jac Charlier, Ric Ohrstrom, and Leslie Balonick, along with the scores of unbelievable change agents who are building the Police, Treatment, and Community Collaborative (PTACC). These pioneers for change are unselfishly and creatively changing the way this nation and other countries around the world address deflection and pre-arrest diversion issues for people with mental health and substance use disorders.

There would be no pioneering programs in the jails, prisons, and community corrections settings in which my companies delivered services if not for the dedicated staff of Valle Management Associates, Inc., Right Turn, Inc., and AdCare Criminal Justice Services, Inc. To the following program services leaders, administrators, teachers, and managers, I thank you: Roger Allen, Michelle Almeda, Michelle Alsup, Lois Arthur, Ed Bleu, Tommie Bower, Dr. Bob Cherney, Eric Dorman, Dr. Maryanne Farkas, Bill Ferney, Anne Gavin, Allen Gaskell, Helen Hines, Eileen Hines, Maureen Kenny-Woodworth, Roberta Kossow, Doreen LeBeau, Dr. Paul Lemieux, Danni Lopes, Dave Lundrigan, Dr. Patrice

Muchowski, Monte Pearse, Dr. Sally Rogers, John Scanlon, Jen Smith, Peter Sullivan, Dr. Ben Thompson, and Dianne Urany.

To my go-to persons for anything and everything, a special shoutout to Gail Farrand at Valle Management Associates, Inc. and Right Turn, Inc., before I joined AdCare, and Lisa-Talbot Lundrigan, chief operating officer for AdCare Criminal Justice Services, Inc. Gail and Lisa were the glue that kept the companies functioning, always met deadlines even on the most important of holidays and vacation periods, never said no to a challenge, kept our contracting agency and customers happy and the staff feeling valued and nurtured, and covered for my flaws and limited social niceties, always doing so with kindness, humor, and grace. Thank you. You are special humans.

For the nearly twenty-five years that I served as president and CEO of AdCare Criminal Justice Services, a sister company of AdCare Hospital (MA), I worked for and with several great colleagues and friends. I especially wish to thank David Hillis, Sr.; Dr. Patrice Muchowski; Jeff Hillis; David Hillis, Jr.; Susan Hillis; Dave Navin; and Dr. Ron Pike as well as the AdCare Hospital Board of Directors for the guidance even when the business trends were challenging.

I would like to acknowledge and express my appreciation to several "friends of Grace House" who gave selflessly of their time and talents to the Grace House residents: Bonnie Alcott supported many of the men by improving their job seeking skills and by providing countless hours of free counseling services; Lance

McCarthy unselfishly devoted his time to enhancing the computer capabilities at the house and currently volunteers his time and talents to the nonprofit organization I founded, the Grace House Institute; Michael Farrand provided employment and support for several Grace House residents when he founded his own freight forwarding business; Russel and Andi Pergament, who gave huge behind-the-scenes emotional and financial support; Pastor Bob Dibbs and the Marblehead Community Church, who unconditionally embraced the Grace House residents; Mary Valle, for her many years of volunteer services as a bookkeeper for Grace House and the Grace House Institute; and my daughter, Marissa, who was active in supporting the community meetings at the house as a young teenager and, as an adult, continues her support of my calling by volunteering her time as a board member of the Grace House Institute. Her creative writing talents were of immeasurable help to me, so much so that I asked her to collaborate with me on this book.

I also want to acknowledge my very dear friends Dr. David DiCicco, Dr. Vicki DiCicco, Dr. Dennis Humphrey, Jared and Amy Noering, and Nat and Joy Wordell for providing constant emotional support, interest, encouragement, and guidance to me over the years as I have shared the vision and my struggles in writing this book; to Dr. David Leveille, my dean of students at Barrington College (RI); my siblings and their families, Dan Valle, Dr. David Valle, Tom Valle, Lois Ann Devaney, and Dr. Jim Valle, who were always faithful and interested supporters of their brother's calling in both words and deeds; my cousin Dr. Tim Engelmann and his wife, Dr. Kim Engelmann, for their feedback and guidance in the direction and content of this book; my Hawthorne Group, consisting of Dr. Dave Denune, Bill Mantzoukas, and Dr. Tony Spartos for the many special luncheons and interesting conversations that spanned decades; Dave Gardner and the savvy and salty sailing crew of the *Solstice*; and my Den-Robin neighborhood friends on Cape Cod (Brewster, MA) for their never-ending interest in Grace House and in my story.

And finally, I thank Jude Berman, Steve Kuhn, and Ed Levy, who were always prompt and spot on in their editing, review, and comments. Jude was exceptional in the multitasking roles she played. They are invaluable resources to me. My thanks as well to Laura Duggan of Nicasio Press. And my utmost thanks and appreciation to Pat Dumas, not only for your attention to all things grammar and your helpful feedback but also for the many hours of fun and laughter we shared throughout this latest phase of my writing and publication journey. You got me to the finish line. Words cannot express my gratitude.

APPENDIX 1
RESOURCES

Addiction Policy Forum, https://www.addictionpolicy.org

Alcoholics Anonymous, https://www.alcoholicsanonymous.com

C4 Recovery Foundation, https://www.c4recoveryfoundation.org

Cape Cod Symposium on Addictive Disorders, https://capecodsymposium.com

DB Recovery Resources, https://www.dbrecoveryresources.com

Engineering and Software Development Services, https://www.dvlup.com

Narcotics Anonymous, https://www.na.org

National Alliance for Recovery Residences, https://www.narronline.org

National Association for Children of Addiction, https://www.nacoa.org

National Sober Living Association, https://www.nationalsoberliving.org

Partnership to End Addiction, https://drugfree.org/

Police Treatment and Community Collaborative, https://www.ptaccollaborative.org

Prison Policy Initiative, https://www.prisonpolicy.org

Substance Abuse and Mental Health Services Administration, https://samhsa.gov

Team Sharing Inc., https://www.teamsharinginc.org

Therapeutic Communities of America, https://www.tcanet.org

United Kingdom/European Symposium on Addictive Disorders, https://www.dbrecoveryresources.com

Vera Institute of Justice, https://www.vera.org

APPENDIX 2
ACCOUNTABILITY
HOW WE CAN BREAK THE CYCLE OF RE-OFFENDING

Dr. Steve Valle, Guest Speaker
President and CEO
AdCare Criminal Justice Services
AdCare Hospital, Worcester, MA USA

International Meeting
United Kingdom and European Symposium on Addiction
Disorders (UKESAD) Conference

House of Lords
All-Party Parliamentary Group on Drugs Misuse
Rt Hon Lord Mancroft, Vice-Chair
London, England, May 12, 2010

Good afternoon, ladies and gentlemen.

It is fitting that my comments today regarding accountability, offender change, and recovery, like so many of America's positive social movements, are British in origin. British physician Maxwell Jones at the end of World War II pioneered the concept of peer-to-peer recovery, which is at the core of the Accountability Model of change for offenders with addiction.

It was Dr. Jones who first envisioned that patients could meaningfully contribute to their own treatment by empowering them to be accountable to one another. By employing peer driven, structured activities, Dr. Jones ushered in a new methodology for promoting pro-social values and creating large-scale social and psychological changes.

The success enjoyed by the early British therapeutic communities greatly influenced the development of prison-based treatment interventions in the U.S., and in particular, the Accountability Training® model that has evolved over the past twenty-five years in my work with offenders who have alcohol and/or drug problems.

Great Britain and the United States share many common core values rooted in our love for freedom and democracy, and in an unwavering belief in the inherent dignity and potential of all of our citizens. We also share in the many challenges presented by a democratic society that respects individual choice and responsibility as we attempt to balance the needs and rights of the individual with what is best for the collective good of society.

Foremost among the social challenges we share is the pervasive availability of highly addictive drugs, including alcohol, and the medical, social, and economic problems caused by addiction to these substances. All of us in this room are joined by a common human experience—we know of someone, likely close to us, who has an addiction problem. And many of us know of someone involved in the criminal justice system because of alcohol and or drug problems.

In America and in Great Britain, our prison systems are in a state of crisis driven in large part to the overcrowding caused by an inmate population that is addicted to drugs.

Consider the following facts:

- More than half of the prison population in England and Wales comprises prisoners with serious drug problems. In the U.S., more than 65 percent (1.5 million) meet the medical criteria for alcohol and other drug abuse and addiction.
- In both countries, our prisons are seriously overcrowded. And in both countries, we are beset with an exasperating cycle of re-offending (over 60 percent).
- The costs to our criminal justice systems are staggering—in the US, over 70 billion dollars a year. This is draining vital resources that are needed in other areas such as education, healthcare, and national security.
- And, according to the media (*USA Today*), drug misuse is now directly related to the national

security of both of our nations. The "Taliban and other insurgents have been using proceeds from the drug trade to fund their insurgency."[39]

In both countries, we send offenders to prison to be accountable for their crimes and to change their behavior. But the evidence is clear, we have failed to break the cycle of re-offending, and for this we all are accountable.

How is this so?

"The tragedy is that we know how to stop spinning this costly and inhumane revolving door.... It starts with acknowledging the fact that addiction is a disease for which... effective treatment programs exist."[40]

Groundbreaking discoveries about the brain have revolutionized our understanding of drug addiction. As a result of scientific research, we know that addiction is a disease that affects both brain and behavior.[41] Despite knowing that addiction is a chronic, relapse-prone disease of the brain, we fail to address it adequately in our criminal justice systems. Because addiction is chronic and compulsive in nature, it does not stop at the prison door.

Now consider these facts:

- Less than 15 percent of the prison population receives any type of treatment for their drug problem, and fewer receive evidence-based care (11 percent in U.S. in 2006—same as in 1996). It is a nagging fact over 95 percent of all prisons will return to the community.
- Offenders who participate and complete evidence-based treatment in prison, and continue with care in

the community, will re-offend at a rate significantly lower than those who just do the time and are released to the streets with no treatment. Numerous studies have made it clear: if we provide evidence-based treatment to offenders, we will reduce re-offending from 10 to 40 percent.
- For every dollar/pound spent on addiction treatment an estimated savings of 12 dollars/pounds in reduced substance-related crime and criminal justice and health care costs will result.
- And now, recently released data from the National Center on Addiction and Substance Abuse at Columbia University "if all inmates with substance use disorders who are not receiving treatment were provided evidenced-based treatment and aftercare, we would break even in one year if just 10 percent of those receiving such services remained substance and crime free and employed. For each succeeding year that these inmates remained substance and crime free and employed, the nation would reap an economic benefit of $90,953 per inmate in reduced crime, lower arrest, prosecution, incarceration and health care costs, and economic benefits from employment. That's a return on investment that would satisfy even the greediest Wall Street bankers."[42]

We all are acutely aware that we are in the midst of a global financial crisis. At a recent international conference on the world's financial condition, it was stated: "The financial crisis of 2008 morphed into an economic crisis during 2009 and has resulted in a governmental crisis in 2010...there is a lack of national or global leadership on these issues which begs the question of whether the government crisis of 2010 will morph into a social crisis."[43]

It's not hyperbole to ask ourselves, "Could we now be on the precipice of a social crisis as well <u>because</u> of our lack of accountability?"

The Accountability Paradigm: Lessons Learned From the Offender

Significant research exists that has repeatedly indicated we now know, with certainty, what works in reducing recidivism of offenders with addiction problems. We know we can reduce recidivism from 10 to 40 percent and get a 12:1 return on our investment. This is what the science of addiction prevention and treatment tells us.

But I would like to share with you what practice has taught me over my twenty-five-year career in working with offenders with alcohol and/or drug problems, and at times, living with them. It is this: the efficacy of science principles, wonderful as they are, are limited and often fall short because of the social and cultural gap that exists between the professional practitioner and the life of the alcoholic/drug addicted offender. Our world is vastly different from theirs.

What we study in the classroom; what we have written in our cherished textbooks, curriculum, and manuals; and what we learn in our offices is far removed from the reality of the drug culture and the day-to-day struggles of survival on the streets; or in the lonely closet of guilt, shame, and denial for those not yet ready to surrender, or who haven't yet been caught.

We can study it and glean essential principles for change from our professional resources, but in my view only another alcoholic or drug addicted offender, him or herself truly knows what it is like to live in the skin of an addict. And they can translate their experience, strength, and hope, in a manner that makes a connection beyond language with another sick, suffering, and despairing alcoholic/addict who desperately wants to change but doesn't believe that they can. I've often heard, "Everyone has given up on me, Doc. I might as will give up on me too."

When hope is lost, despair sets in. A human being in despair is frightening and dangerous for all. But in the power of example and in the energy of hope that lives in a recovering peer group member, wearing the same color jump suit and sleeping in the same cell, living with the same demeaning prison conditions day in and day out, but still determined to get recovery and to change, there is unmatched credibility and depth of empathic understanding from one's peer.

Hope is restored because they see it in the eyes and in the actions of their peer who is living recovery and change right before their own eyes. In the power of example, hope lives and prevails.

Thus, I have learned from offenders with addiction problems—which I believe your Dr. Maxwell Jones had the vision to see over sixty years ago—that the peer group can translate our science-based principles into their language and culture much more effectively than can most of us.

And this is where we are accountable: it is our role to capture, to harness, and to direct the enormous energy and power that exists in the offender peer group consisting of those who do want to change. They can't do it alone, and neither can you or I.

So, it is from the peer group of recovering offenders with addiction that I have discovered what I have termed "the formula for change." It is this: Accountability + Respect + Community = Recovery & Change.

This formula for change is actually a paradigm, a way of thinking and looking at how we can most effectively deliver science-based principles to the offender population. The essence of this Accountability Model is that it is peer driven.

Unless respect can be established, unless accountability to one another is practiced, and unless we have the support of community, our success will be limited. But, if we can wrap our cherished science-based principles around this paradigm, and teach the offender how to teach one another, we have a better chance of imbedding pro-social change into the mindset and the lifestyle of the offender.

It is within the offenders' peer group that lie the solution and the support for turning one's life around. We can be extremely helpful as coaches, teachers, and facilitators. But the offenders' peer group is the most powerful medium for the message of hope, recovery, and change. And they are always available.

So, by organizing, guiding, and shaping the offenders' peer group while in prison, and continuing it in the community, offenders will learn from each other, with modeling and direction provided by staff, much quicker and more meaningfully than from professionals alone.

I'd like to make one last point and then illustrate it with a brief story.

What we have learned from offenders is that accountability is a concept that is not natural for many. Because of the intergenerational aspect of addiction and criminality, many offenders need to be taught what it means to be accountable. We expect offenders to learn to be responsible, but often, they are not able to make the desired response society expects of them. So accountability needs to be first taught, and then experienced. As the offenders learn this by being immersed in peer-led but staff-directed therapeutic communities that are pro-social, the ingredients for change and recovery are experienced and reinforced. Respect, accountability, and the value of community are integrated. The result is pro-social behavior change and meaningful recovery.

To illustrate how the concept of accountability is one that needs to be learned by the offender, and that often the best teachers of it can come from unexpected sources, I'd like to close with the following story:

> The man in the shadows waited until the family got all of its belongings into the car, checked everything, had the car loaded up, and pulled away for their summer vacation. The man in the shadows waited until it was dark, and then went to the front door of the house and rang the bell. When there was no answer, this man, seasoned thief that he was, had no

trouble picking the lock and getting inside. As a precaution he called out to the darkness, "Is anybody home?"

He was stunned when he heard a voice reply, "I see you, and Jesus sees you."

Terrified, the thief called out, "Who's there?"

And again the voice came back, "I see you and Jesus sees you."

So the thief switched on his flashlight toward the direction of the voice and was immediately relieved to see a caged parrot who recited once more, "I see you, and Jesus sees you." He laughed to himself and then went to the wall and threw on the light switch. Then he saw it. Beneath the parrot's cage was a huge Doberman pinscher. The parrot said, "Attack, Jesus, attack.[44]

The offender in the story quickly learned one of the principles of accountability—we all answer, at some point, to an authority greater than ourselves.

We hold the offender accountable for the crime, as we should. But all of us are accountable for doing what we know can break the cycle of re-offending and also result in significant cost savings for the taxpayer—effective, long-term, treatment for the disease of addiction.

The offender with an addiction problem needs the help of others to change. Addiction is a disease of isolation, the recovery and change process involves re-establishing connections in one's community. The formula for change does not only involve the offender. It is for us as well.

We are accountable to one another because our societies and mutual well-being requires us to be mindful of others. Authority and structure and boundaries are essential for our societies to function cohesively. We cherish the core principle of respect for the dignity, worth, and potential of every human being. Including those individuals who make mistakes. Especially when those mistakes are the result of a chronic disease that has been left untreated.

And because we live in community, we need each other. In the words of your Sir Richard Branson, "Everything is linked."

When offenders have the opportunity to learn better, and the teaching and training to know better, many will—as the evidence indicates—do better.

Perhaps the time has come for all of us to be accountable also, to do our part to break the cycle of re-offending. The offender with addiction is accountable to change, to take right action, and so are we.

Thank you.

ABOUT THE AUTHOR

Stephen K. Valle is a recognized leader and international expert in the addiction, criminal justice, and mental health fields. In 1993, he was nominated by Senator Harold E. Hughes to serve as director of the Federal Substance Abuse and Mental Health Services Administration (SAMHSA) in the Clinton administration. In 2010, he was invited to address Parliament's House of Lords All-Party Parliamentary Group on Drug Misuse regarding prison reform and addiction issues in the United Kingdom and in the United States.

Dr. Valle is the founder of Accountability Training, a behavior change model for offenders with addiction. In 1996, he converted his former home in Lynn, MA, into a sober residence and founded Grace House. Grace House was the first Oxford House for people without a home and recently released offenders with addiction and co-occurring problems in the state. The conceptual framework of his Accountability Training model grew out of his unique connection with the residents of Grace House and with other offenders in the many programs he established throughout the country.

A licensed psychologist and licensed alcohol and drug abuse counselor, Dr. Valle was president and CEO of AdCare Criminal Justices Services, an affiliate of AdCare Hospital, in Worcester, MA for twenty-five years. He is currently chairman of the board of Valle Management Associates, Inc., an international addictions and behavioral health consulting company. He is the author of over a dozen journal articles and of *Alcoholism Counseling: Issues for an Emerging Profession*, and was the editor of *Drunk Driving in America: Strategies and Approaches to Treatment* and an associate editor of the *Alcoholism Treatment Quarterly*.

Endnotes

1. *Merriam-Webster*, s.v. "solstice," accessed February 7, 2019, from http://www.merriam-webster.com/dictionary.

2. Cynthia Bourgeault, *The Holy Trinity and the Law of Three: Discovering the Radical Truth at the Heart of Christianity* (Boston: Shambhala, 2013), 4, 215.

3. Richard Rohr, "The Law of Three," *Daily Meditations*, Thursday, May 16, 2019, https://cac.org/daily-meditations/the-law-of-three-2019-05-16/.

4. Bourgeault, *The Holy Trinity*, 206.

5. "'185aDay' Campaign to Raise Awareness of Drug Overdose Deaths," Addiction Policy Forum, March 12, 2020, https://www.addictionpolicy.org/post/185aday-campaign-to-raise-awareness-of-drug-overdose-deaths; Carlie Porterfield, "Opioid Overdose Deaths Cost U.S. Economy $1 Trillion A Year, Study Finds," *Forbes*, February 8, 2022, https://www.forbes.com/sites/carlieporterfield/2022/02/08/opioid-overdose-deaths-cost-us-economy-1-trillion-a-year-study-finds/?sh=33af6d6753b7.

6. Brian Mann, "Overdose Deaths in U.S. Top 100,000 for the First Time, NPR, November 17, 2021, https://www.npr.org/2021/11/17/1056484849/drug-overdose-deaths-100000-us.

7. The White House, "Executive Order on Imposing Sanctions on Foreign Persons Involved in the Global Illicit Drug Trade," December 15, 2021, https://www.whitehouse.gov/briefing-room/presidential-actions/2021/12/15/executive-order-on-imposing-sanctions-on-foreign-persons-involved-in-the-global-illicit-drug-trade/.

8. US Department of Health and Human Services, "U.S. Surgeon General Issues Advisory on Youth Mental Health Crisis Further Exposed by COVID-19 Pandemic, December 7, 2021, https://www.hhs.gov/about/news/2021/12/07/us-surgeon-general-issues-advisory-on-youth-mental-health-crisis-further-exposed-by-covid-19-pandemic.html.

9. Centers for Disease Control, "Death Rate Maps & Graphs," last modified June 2, 2022, https://www.cdc.gov/drugoverdose/deaths/index.html.

10. Mic. 6:8 (King James Version).

11. Peter Carlson, "The Oxford House Experiment," *Washington Post*, November 12, 1989, https://www.washingtonpost.com/archive/lifestyle/magazine/1989/11/12/the-oxford-house-experiment/f48142e1-877e-469e-bf1f-aa6aec605e56/.

12. "History and Accomplishments," Oxford House, n.d., https://oxfordhouse.org/oxford_house_history.

13. Anne Lamont, "12 Truths I Learned From Life and Writing," TED, June 9, 2017, YouTube video, 15:45, https://www.ted.com/talks/anne_lamott_12_truths_i_learned_from_life_and_writing?language=so.

14. Mimi Silbert, "Keynote Address" (Boston Conference on Substance Abuse Treatment for Offender Population, Boston, MA, 1986). Mimi Silber is cofounder of Delancey Street Foundation, San Francisco, CA.

15. "Our President," Delancey Street Foundation, 2007, http://www.delanceystreetfoundation.org/presidentfull.php.

16. Kris Olsen, "At 89, Ex-Quincy Judge Still Seeking New Challenges," *Massachusetts Lawyers Weekly Daily*, August 5, 2022, https://masslawyersweekly.com/2022/08/05/at-89-ex-quincy-judge-not-ready-to-slow-down/.

17. Bruce Carruth and Stephen K. Valle, *Drunk Driving in America: Strategies and Approaches to Treatment* (New York: Routledge, 1986).

18. Therapeutic Communities of America, http://www.tcanet.org/.

19. Rohr, "A Stirring of the Soul," *Daily Meditations*, March 1, 2022, https://cac.org/daily-meditations/a-stirring-of-the-soul-2022-03-01/.

20. Desmond Tutu, *No Future Without Forgiveness* (New York: Doubleday, 1999), 31.

21. *Restoring the Shack*, directed by Stephan Blinn, featuring William Paul Young, season 1, episode 1, 3:15, Amazon Prime, Bridgestone Multimedia Group, 2020.

22. Rohr, "One Diverse Family," *Daily Meditations*, February 8, 2022, https://cac.org/daily-meditations/members-of-one-diverse-family-2022-02-08/.

23. BOTEC Analysis Corporation, *A Study on the Habilitation of Chronic Offenders in a Massachusetts House of Correction*, 2003. Barnstable County Sheriff's Department, Bourne, MA.

24. Richard Branson, *Screw Business As Usual: Turning Capitalism Into a Force for Good* (New York: Penguin Random House, 2011), 297.

25. Piero Ferrucci and Dalai Lama, *The Power of Kindness: The Unexpected Benefits of Leading a Compassionate Life* (New York: Penguin Random House, 2016), 95.

26. Stephen Valle and L. Talbot-Lundrigan, "Keynote Presentation" (American Correctional Association Annual Meeting, Galveston, TX, 2012).

27. Roger Allen, *Shock Program Curriculum* (Barnstable, MA: Barnstable County Sheriff's Department, 2007).

28. Pema Chödrön, *When Things Fall Apart: Heart Advice for Difficult Times* (Boston, MA: Shambhala Publications, 1997), 1.

29. David Sheff, *Beautiful Boy: A Father's Journey Through His Son's Addiction* (Boston: Houghton Mifflin, 2008) 145.

30. Sheff, *Beautiful Boy*.

31. The National Center on Addiction and Substance Abuse at Columbia University, *Behind Bars II: Substance Abuse and America's Prison Population* (New York: Author), February 2010.

32. "Don't Stop Believin'," by Steve Perry and Neal Schon, on Journey, *Escape*, released October 19, 1981, Columbia Records.

33. Reverend Jennifer Zogg, Church of the Epiphany, East Providence, RI, April 2020.

34. Isa. 61:3 (King James Version).

35. Eric Bock, "Addiction Is a Complex Brain Disease, Says Volkow," *NIH Record*, 72, no. 2 (January 24, 2020), https://nihrecord.nih.gov/2020/01/24/addiction-complex-brain-disease-says-volkow.

36. April Pattavina and Ronald P. Corbett, "How Smartphone Technology Can Link the Theoretical, Policy, and Practical Contexts of Community Supervision Reform: Voices From the Field," *Victims and Offenders*, 14, no. 7 (September 2, 2019): 777–92, https://doi.org/10.1080/15564886.2019.1659894.

37. Team Sharing, Inc., 2022, https://www.teamsharinginc.org/. Team Sharing's Massachusetts Chapter is located at 289 Elm Street, Suite 105, Marlborough, MA, 01752.

38. Eccles. 3:1 (King James Version).

39. "From Poppies to Wheat," Marine Corps News Room, https://marine-corps-news.com/2009/03/.

40. Joseph A. Califano Jr., "Criminally Unjust: Why America's Prison Policy Needs Repair, *America Magazine*, May 24, 2010, https://www.americamagazine.org/politics-society/2010/05/24/califano-criminally-unjust-why-america-prison-policy-needs-repair.

41. Nora Volkow, NIDA, 2010.

42. National Center on Addiction and Substance Abuse at Columbia University, *Behind Bars II: Substance Abuse and America's Prison Population*, February 2010, ii, https://www.prisonlegalnews.org/media/publications/Behind%20Bars%20II%20-%20Substance%20Abuse%20and%20Americas%20Prison%20Population%2C%20CASA%2C%202010.pdf.

43. Carol McMullen President, Eastern Wealth Management, Eastern Bank, Lynn, MA.

44. William J. Bausch, *A World of Stories* (Mystic, CT: Twenty-Third Publications, 1999), 391.

CPSIA information can be obtained
at www.ICGtesting.com
Printed in the USA
JSHW052054091222
34346JS00001B/4